C000171183

# THORPE ST ANDREW
*A Revised History*

TREVOR NUTHALL

First published 2002 as
Thorpe St Andrew – A History

This revised edition first published 2014 by

Trevor Nuthall
52 Cambridge Street
Norwich NR2 2BB

**ISBN 978-0-9543359-1-5**

Typeset & printed by Catton Print of Norwich

# CONTENTS

### III: From the present and old churches to Barber Place

### IV: From No. 103 Yarmouth Road to School Avenue

### V: From Thorpe Mews to Primrose Crescent

### VI: From Pound Lane to the Griffin

*VII: From Meadowlands to Boundary Lane*

APPENDIX 1
THORPE MANOR

APPENDIX 2

APPENDIX 3

APPENDIX 4

## LIST OF ILLUSTRATIONS AND MAPS                    Page

*Front cover:* Thorpe Hall from a drawing by T Higham of about 1818
*Back cover:* The present church, the Buck and a building west of No. 63 Yarmouth Road, in 1905

### Plates

**Maps (based on originals drawn by Brian Larkman)**

# INTRODUCTION

## Outline

This book outlines briefly where Thorpe St Andrew is and its relationship with the original parish of Thorpe-next-Norwich or Thorpe Episcopi. The history of Thorpe is then traced through describing an imaginary two-mile journey along Yarmouth Road from Harvey Lane to Boundary Lane (just beyond St Andrew's Park). Many of the buildings and lanes along the way are described and linked with the historical development of Thorpe, concentrating predominantly on Thorpe before 1850, but including some information about later buildings. Finally, the appendices tell the story of the lordship of the manor of Thorpe and describe the important role of Mousehold Heath. In addition, there are maps of Thorpe in about 1600, about 1750 and 1800 and details are given of the sources used in compiling this history.

Something about the history of Thorpe before 1500 can be found in "The original church and settlement", "Thorpe Hall - Description and history before 1535" and "No. 127 Yarmouth Road etc". The major changes that happened in the 16th century are set out in "The old church and the movement of the settlement" and "Dussindale". The latter was the site of the 16th century battle that ended Kett's Rebellion. The history and development of Thorpe Hall and St Andrew's Hospital are described in detail. (St Andrew's Hospital is now "St Andrew's Park" and "St Andrew's Business Park"). There are also descriptions of the three churches of Thorpe St Andrew ("the present church", "the old church" and "the original church"). Also described are the green, common, public houses, poorhouses and all significant buildings that stand or have stood along Yarmouth Road between Harvey Lane and Boundary Lane. In addition, the story of Yarmouth Road itself has been traced as well as that of the lanes and tracks that link or have linked with it, including Yarmouth Way.

Many sources have been used but particularly significant have been maps, especially:
- a 1589 map of Mousehold Heath ("the 1589 Mousehold map"),
- a circa 1600 map of Mousehold Heath, showing sheepwalks ("the 1600 Mousehold map" - the Thorpe St Andrew section of this is reproduced as Plate 40 in Appendix 3 below),
- two sketch maps of between 1700 and 1731 ("the 1700 / 1731 sketch maps"),
- a 1718 map of "the Fould Courses of Plumstead, Lumners Great Close and Fould Course, lying in Plumstead, Sprowston and Thorp" ("the 1718 map"),
- an 1800 draft enclosure map of Thorpe by R Chasteney ("the 1800 enclosure map"),
- an 1825 map of rivers between Norwich and Reedham, with names of owners of adjacent lands ("the 1825 river map"),
- an 1841 tithe map for Thorpe ("the 1841 tithe map") and
- Ordnance Survey maps of the 1880s and later.

In about 1760 Thomas Bardwell painted "A Prospect of Trowse Hall, Norwich". The two figures in the foreground appear to be William Money and his son John, who later became General Money. In the background is the earliest view of Thorpe St Andrew. In this book, I have referred to this as "Bardwell's 1760 painting".

Use has been made of information in the Norfolk Historic Environment Record maintained by the Norfolk Historic Environment Service. Details of all sources are listed in Appendix 4.

# Where is Thorpe?

Thorpe St Andrew has only been the official name of the parish since 1954. Previously it was known as Thorpe-next-Norwich and, prior to 1535, Thorpe Episcopi or Bishop's Thorpe. Since Norwich expanded in the 15th or 16th century, Thorpe has been a divided parish. It has been split between the part of Thorpe in Norwich (Thorpe Hamlet) and the part of Thorpe in Broadland (now known as Thorpe St Andrew). The dividing line is Harvey Lane. To the west is the city, to the east the county.

Thorpe Hamlet is defined by the River Wensum to the west and south and part of Heartsease Lane, Harvey Lane and a line just east of Frogs Hall Lane (east of No. 129 Thorpe Road) to the east. The official southern boundary of Mousehold Heath ("Beech Drive" - not far south of the east-west stretch of Gurney Road) forms much of the northern boundary.

The northern limit of Thorpe St Andrew runs along Plumstead Road East and the southern edge of the Greenborough Road area. (Until 1950 it went as far north as what is now Rider Haggard Road and Lishman Road on the Heartsease Estate). To the east are the parishes of Great Plumstead and Postwick and here the boundary runs from Green Lane North (off Plumstead Road East) to Boundary Lane (off Yarmouth Road). To the south the River Yare is the boundary. To the west Thorpe St Andrew meets Thorpe Hamlet.

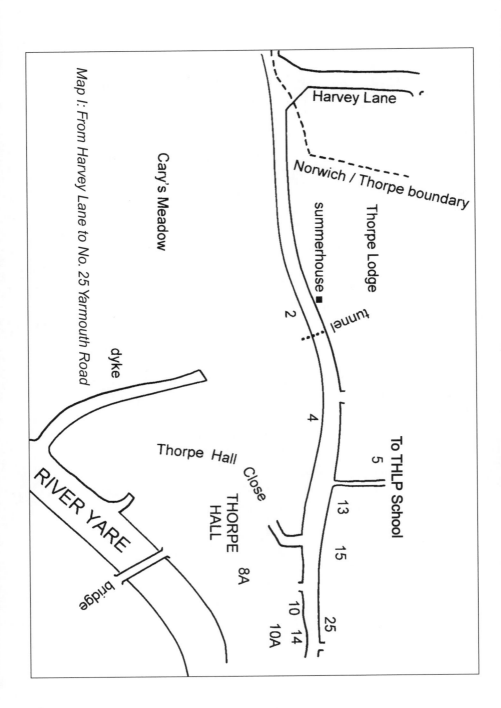

Map I: From Harvey Lane to No. 25 Yarmouth Road

Harvey Lane

Norwich / Thorpe boundary

Thorpe Lodge

summerhouse

tunnel

2

Cary's Meadow

dyke

4

Thorpe Hall

Close

THORPE HALL

8A

To THLP School

5

13

15

10  14

25

10A

RIVER YARE

bridge

# Yarmouth Road, Thorpe St Andrew

## I: From Harvey Lane to No. 25 Yarmouth Road

## HARVEY LANE

Harvey Lane is named after John Harvey who lived at Thorpe Lodge during the first half of the 19th century (see "Thorpe Lodge" below). By the 15th century it was the boundary line between Thorpe and Norwich. A draft Norwich charter of 1461 mentions a boundary cross that stood where Yarmouth Way crossed Harvey Lane. This was by the present junction with Rockland Drive.

As well as the boundary line between Thorpe and Norwich, in the 15th and 16th centuries, Harvey Lane was the eastern boundary of an oak wood that had been part of Thorpe Wood – see "The oak wood (now Lion Wood)" in Appendix 2 below. However, it appears that until the 13th or 14th century woodland may have stretched from Harvey Lane as far east as Dale's Loke / Bishop's Close (see "Thorpe Hall - Description and history before 1535" below).

Until 1801, Harvey Lane entered Mousehold Heath where the southern boundaries of the gardens of Gordon Avenue are. As late as the 1840s, it was referred to as Rose's Lane, presumably after the Rose family who owned property in Thorpe in the early 18th century. The will of Matthew Rose senior of Thorpe was proved in 1707.

In 1819 the southern end of Harvey Lane was moved westwards to enable John Harvey to extend the grounds around Thorpe Lodge (see "Thorpe Lodge" below). It meant that this part of the road no longer followed Norwich's eastern boundary.

# THORPE LODGE
## NOW BROADLAND DISTRICT COUNCIL OFFICES

Thorpe Lodge dates from about 1800 and has five bays with sashes. Until at least the 1920s it had two and a half (rather than two) storeys and a three-bay east wing that made the building almost symmetrical (Plate 1). It was built by John Harvey, who moved from Norwich to Thorpe in about 1800. He was a banker and textile manufacturer and had been mayor of Norwich in 1792. Harvey introduced the manufacture of shawls into Norwich in 1791. He was prominent in the local militia and was known as Colonel Harvey.

The 1600 Mousehold map shows that there had been a house on the site from at least that date. A 1767 manor court entry describes the site boundaries. To the north was the bottom of a hill called the Common Hill or the Sugar Loaf Hill. To the east was the Pound Close, otherwise called the Claypit Close, that belonged to the lord of the manor. To the south was the highway (Yarmouth Road). To the west was Rose's Lane (see "Harvey Lane" above).

*Plate 1 : Thorpe Lodge in 1924 from a sale catalogue, showing the building before it was altered.*

Bardwell's 1760 painting shows a fine house on the Thorpe Lodge site with three storeys and four bays. There are walls projecting from both sides of the house and then running southwards to Yarmouth Road. To the west of the site, next to Harvey Lane, is a much smaller building.

In 1806 Harvey acquired the Thorpe Hall estate from his father in law, Sir Roger Kerrison. In 1819 Harvey extended the grounds of Thorpe Lodge to the west and to the south. He did this by diverting Yarmouth Road southwards (as far as the summerhouse opposite No. 2 Yarmouth Road) and Harvey Lane westwards. An 1819 plan shows the old Harvey Lane running south and then the old Yarmouth Road heading west along the Norwich boundary. Following the extension of his grounds, Harvey built the "crinkle crankle" wall that now runs from near the bottom of Harvey Lane to where Eden Close joins Harvey Lane.

In 1833 Robberds described how in 1808 the "large fir trees" in the wood west of Harvey Lane (which he called "Thorpe Old Grove") were cut down. Looking back to the early 19th century, Hardy described how Harvey had "bought the whole of Thorpe Grove, enlarged the Park about his own house, built a house with grounds for his second son, and by the mere sale of timber on the estate, reimbursed himself for the price paid." (Harvey's second son was George Harvey. Part of his house, "The Grove", may now be incorporated in the house of that name that adjoins No. 4 Matlock Road, off Thorpe Road).

Between 1806 and 1818, Harvey reduced the area of woodland west of Harvey Lane from 61 acres to 21 acres (see "The oak wood (now Lion Wood)" in Appendix 2 below). The reduction included 34 acres west of the track that runs between Wellesley Avenue South and Wellesley Avenue North and about 5.5 acres east of that track.

Harvey was involved in property development and the replanning of Thorpe Hamlet following the building of Carrow Bridge and Foundry Bridge in 1810. This included creating the part of Thorpe Road from Foundry Bridge to the junction with Rosary Road and making a road from Carrow Bridge (then at the bottom of Carrow Hill) to Thorpe Road.

Harvey's father, Robert, died in 1816 and left him property in Lingwood and Blofield. It was bequeathed on the basis that Harvey had a life interest and on his death it would pass to his children or to such of them as Harvey decided. In May 1818 Harvey secured a private Act of Parliament, under which these trusts were transferred from the property in Lingwood and Blofield to the Thorpe Hall estate, including the woodland west of Harvey Lane. Over the next twenty years, Harvey divided the Thorpe Hall estate between three of his children. Sir Robert John Harvey, his eldest son, was given most of the land west of Harvey Lane. (Here he built what became Mousehold House). Harriot Blakiston, Harvey's sixth daughter, was given Thorpe Hall (see "Thorpe Hall – Thorpe Hall from 1535" below). The rest was given to Roger Kerrison Harvey, Harvey's third son.

South-east of Thorpe Lodge and opposite No. 2 Yarmouth Road is an octagonal summerhouse that Harvey built. The 17th century door-frame that used to contain the door to the road is mentioned below

*Plate 2 : Outside the gates of Thorpe Lodge, looking up Yarmouth Road, in about 1910.*

in connection with Thorpe Hall. By 1841 Harvey had turned the summerhouse into a camera obscura. This was a darkened chamber into which light was admitted through a double convex lens forming an image of external objects on paper or glass placed at the focus of the lens.

About 27 yards (25 metres) east of the summerhouse, there is a tunnel running under the road. It is an underground passage between Thorpe Lodge and Thorpe Hall that is now a cave for bats. In 1842 it was described as leading "from the Lawn to the Gardener's Cottage, and Kitchen Garden" (Thorpe Lodge), "to the premises of the Home Farm, and the Boat-houses near the river" (Thorpe Hall). It is a tunnel folly faced with flint and brick and constructed by John Harvey following the fashion of the time. It was refaced in the 1920s.

In a July 1841 account of a bazaar in the grounds of Thorpe Lodge, it was observed that the "tunnel which leads down to the meadows was a source of attraction – it was lighted with coloured lamps and had a novel appearance." Reference is also made to "the greenhouses, conservatories and camera obscura" in the grounds of Thorpe Lodge. Grigor, writing in the same year, also refers to a "grotto, beautifully secluded among the trees".

In Norwich Castle Museum & Art Gallery there is a large painting called *Thorpe Water Frolic - afternoon*. It is by Joseph Stannard and was first exhibited in 1825. Harvey had instigated the water frolic in 1821 partly as a sporting event but more importantly as a social event for the gentry. It was repeated in 1822 when cutters and rowing boats raced for silver cups. In 1823 the event was opened up to the working population of Norwich and the local weavers were given a holiday. 10,000 attended in 1823 and nearly twice that number in 1824. There were clear social distinctions; the gentry amused themselves on the north bank of the river (the Thorpe side) and the working population on the south bank (the Trowse side).

Fawcett (1977) describes Stannard's painting:

> On the left, enclosing Harvey himself, are the members of his family, his guests and the Dragoon Guards band; the ladies show off their fine fashionable dresses and bonnets, the gentlemen wear or flourish top hats. On the right, at the inner bend of the river, are the ordinary citizens, more or less displaying the traits of popular manners.

The event was repeated several times during the 1820s and revived in 1835. There were similar regattas in the 1840s (organised by Robert Cattermole of Thorpe Gardens - now the Rushcutters) and also in the 1850s.

*Plate 3 :Looking down Yarmouth Road from the site of No.2 Yarmouth Road, in about 1910.*

# BETWEEN THORPE LODGE AND NUMBER 25 YARMOUTH ROAD

The oldest building between Thorpe Lodge and No. 25 Yarmouth Road may be No. 13 Yarmouth Road (Ivy Cottage). At the time of the Harvey sale in 1842, it included "Wheelwright's, Carpenter's and Blacksmith's shops, Sawpit-house" and "Timber Yard". It does not appear on the 1825 river map. The Norfolk Historic Environment Record describes it as an early 19th century flint cottage with brick quoins, window surrounds and a string course at the level of the upper floor. There is a blocked window over the door and one original chimney pot. Map evidence suggests that No.15 Yarmouth Road (Inglehurst) also dates from about the 1830s. In 1842 it was called Vine Cottage.

West of No. 13 Yarmouth Road is a track. It is clear from the 1800 enclosure map that near where the track meets the road was the site of a small, rectangular pound where stray animals were kept until a fine was paid, see Plate 4 and "Pound Lane" below. The track may mark what was the eastern boundary of the Thorpe Lodge estate. Before Harvey extended the estate as far east as this, the boundary was probably opposite the eastern boundary of No. 2 Yarmouth Road. (This is where Harvey's tunnel goes under the road – see "Thorpe Lodge" above). The estate was encroached upon in about 1850 by Holly Lodge (No. 5 Yarmouth Road) and in about 1860 by Sunny Hill (now No. 7 Yarmouth Road). Sunny Hill was first associated with William H Clabburn, a shawl manufacturer. In the early 1950s Thorpe House School moved there (see also "Old Thorpe House" below). Most of the original building was demolished in the 1970s. In 2010, Thorpe House School came to an end and Sunny Hill became the site of Thorpe House Langley Preparatory School.

Before reaching Thorpe House Langley Preparatory School, the track forks eastwards towards a large house that dates from about 1880. This is No. 11 Yarmouth Road. In 1880 it was known as Belle Vue, a name that was changed in about 1900 to Beech Hill. It was first associated with Hugh Gurney Barclay, a banker. Beech Hill was the home of Langley Preparatory School until 2010, when they moved to the Sunny Hill site.

# THORPE HALL

## Description and history before 1535

On the south side of Yarmouth Road is Thorpe Hall. In 1735/36 Harrison described it as "encompassed with a flint Stone Wall." This implies the wall went right round the site. From the eastern edge of Cary's Meadow, you can see what is left of the flint wall that runs along the east side of the 147 yard (134 metre) dyke or ditch, immediately west of Nos. 16-25 Thorpe Hall Close. This was the western boundary of the site.

Bardwell's 1760 painting shows a stone wall running along the southern boundary near the river, and then turning northwards just before a landing place at the bottom of a lane running between the hall and No. 12 Yarmouth Road. The lane (further west than in 1760) can be seen on the 1800 enclosure map (Plate 4) and in James Stark's "*Thorpe Old Hall, Norwich*" that dates from 1829. The riverside wall would have been a necessary defence against flooding. An 1818 drawing of Thorpe Hall (Higham) (Plate 6) shows a ruined wall south-east of the present hall and running west-south-westwards about 20 yards (18 metres) from the river. The garden walls that in the 1880s ran in the same direction up to a second dyke and then up to the 147 yard (134 metre) dyke (Plate 7) may originally have been continuations of this wall. They started south of the house about 20 yards (18 metres) from the river and joined the western wall referred to above about 60 yards (55 metres) from the river.

Much of the original northern boundary of the site can be seen in the brick and flint wall that forms the present boundary along Yarmouth Road. The original boundary wall may have run from near the eastern boundary of No. 2 Yarmouth Road to the western wall of No. 14 Yarmouth Road. There may have been some angling northwards of the boundary between just east of a point opposite what is now No. 13 Yarmouth Road and No. 14 Yarmouth Road. This is indicated by the change of angle of the wall east of the garden entrance and the old masonry that has been built into it just before Thorpe Hall Close. In addition, it is clear from the manor court records that in 1744 part of this boundary was extended seven yards (six metres) northwards to include what is now No. 10 Yarmouth Road. In the 1980s, the wall was affected by the building of Thorpe Hall Close and the new access to Thorpe Hall. The latter is just west of where the main access to the hall was from the late 18th century until 1841 (Plate 4).

By 1800 there were farm buildings west of the hall. From the 1880s Ordnance Survey map (Plate 7), it is clear there was a farm entrance opposite what is now the modern extension to Thorpe Lodge. There was a track that came in here (across the present site of the Anglian Water pumping station) curving south-eastwards and then eastwards. It would have entered the manor site, north of the 147-yard (134-metre) dyke referred to above. Entry may originally have been through a gateway and would have been into an outer court. To the north were farm buildings and to the south, by 1825, fishponds. In the 1880s,

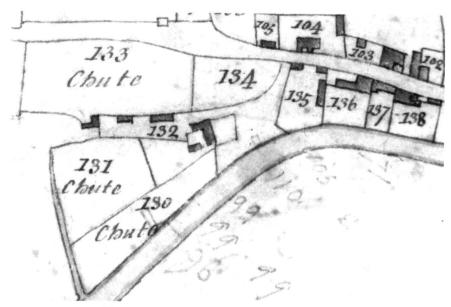

*Plate 4 : Thorpe Hall from the 1800 enclosure map.*

when you entered the outer court, you would have seen to the north a large barn and then a stable and to the south pigsties and, behind them, east of the dyke, two fishponds. Parts of the barn were believed to be medieval.

Until the site was divided in 1838, you could have continued eastwards beyond the barn yard and stable yard, and entered what could be regarded as the inner court. To enter it, you would have crossed a boundary that included the second dyke, which in 1841 was about 67 yards (61 metres) in length, but by the 1880s had been shortened considerably. (What remains of the dyke now seems to be between Nos. 14 and 15 Thorpe Hall Close). As you entered the court, there were buildings on three sides. This is an area occupied today partly by the hall and partly by the property immediately south-west of it (Nos. 7-12 Thorpe Hall Close). Now the only part of the hall that remains is the south wing and part of the west wing. In the 1880s, the south wing would have had a low southern extension that ran down towards the river, thus forming the eastern side of the courtyard. (The southern extension would have run up to the current southern boundary of Thorpe Hall). West of the end of that extension, and forming the southern side of the courtyard was the chapel (Plate 5). (Its site is now outside the current boundary of Thorpe Hall. It is immediately north of 13 Thorpe Hall Close and partly under Nos. 7-12 Thorpe Hall Close). In the 1880s, the low west wing would have continued a little further with a taller extension at its western end. It formed the northern boundary of the yard.

From what can be ascertained from the building, Thorpe Hall may have originated as a 14th century courtyard house. What is now the south wing comprised, from south to north: opposing doorways (forming a screens passage), an open hall (with a chimney on the western side that still exists) and a parlour (with rooms above). The southern extension would have contained service rooms for the storage and preparation of food. An architectural survey suggests that the present west wing of the hall did not originally join the south wing. Until the 1950s or the 1960s the present low west wing was 50% longer again than it is now. The missing western third had a higher and steeper roof than what remains. It appears that the difference in height was because of a fire that badly damaged much of the west wing. It was rebuilt with a much lower roof. This makes it difficult to imagine what it was originally like. The west wing may have contained service rooms.

According to Kent, the chapel on the south side of the yard had five Decorated windows, a fine cross on its western gable, a stone piscina and two finely moulded doors. The mouldings on the doors were very much like those on the door in the north wall of Suckling House, Norwich, to which a date of between 1350 and 1370 was given in 1917. The chapel was demolished in 1936. In 1958 the doors were said to be at Sudeley Hall in Gloucestershire. The east gable cross of Fritton church in Suffolk is said to have come from Thorpe Hall, presumably from the chapel.

A 1535 survey (Supple pages 72-3) describes the hall as the "fermour's dwellynge, with a stable annexed to it at the west end; and with two

*Plate 5 : Thorpe Hall and chapel from a 1920s drawing by Theresa Cubitt.*

barns and pigstyes at the end of them, with the kyl-house" (i.e. a malt-kiln). In 1428/9 10s 10d was spent on a new great table and nearly £5 on roofing the bake-house and hall (Hayes).

The hall was a multi-purpose building. It was primarily a farm run by the bishop's bailiff to provide income and produce for the bishop and his household. It was also the manor house of Thorpe, where the bishop or his officials held the manor court. Other official business was also undertaken there, including the issuing of charters. The earliest charter issued at Thorpe dates from 1206, although at that time the hall may have occupied a different site (see below). In the early 15th century some heresy trials were held at the hall either in the chapel or in the parlour (Tanner). Sometimes the bishop stayed there. According to Hayes, it was Bishop Alnwick's favourite residence in the Norwich area. In 1425 Bishop Wakering died in the house.

Thorpe Hall, as we see it today, probably dates from the first half of the 14th century. There may have been a manor house on the site in the 13th century, but exactly where is not clear. Supple (page 60) refers to there being "considerable foundations". Kent said "some early foundations had been found but never explored". It may have been a timber-framed building without any stone foundations.

Yaxley and Virgoe have suggested that many manor houses are some distance from the original focus point of the settlement, because they were established in the 12th or 13th centuries, when new parts of the parish were being brought into intensive cultivation. They mention Colkirk, "where by 1296 the manor house had been removed from the centre of the village to a moated site on the edge of a large area of heath and woodland nearly a mile to the east of the parish church." All these factors may well have been true at Thorpe, although the manor house may not have moved until the first half of the 14th century.

The shapes of the fields on the 1800 enclosure map suggest that there was a large area of woodland from Harvey Lane eastwards as far as a track now represented by Dale's Loke / Bishop's Close (see "The original church and settlement" and Plate 42 below). This woodland was probably cleared for cultivation in the 13th or 14th century. Thorpe Hall may have been built as the focus of this new agricultural area. It is now clear that it was about a mile from the original church (see "The original church and settlement" below). It is likely that the earlier manor house would have been much closer to the original church. Harper-Bill (document 139) quotes an agreement of 1239 between the bishop of Norwich and the Cathedral Priory under which Mousehold Heath was to be divided into three equal parts. It refers to the two parts nearest the manor (i.e. nearest the manor house) going to the bishop and the third, more distant, part going to the priory. This only makes sense if in 1239 the manor house was near the eastern end of the parish.

There is slight evidence of a building that could have been associated with the new 14th century manor house. In 1735/6 Harrison referred to "a Chappel belonging to the Hall, the remains whereof converted into a Barn, stand upon an eminence opposite to it on the other side of the Street". This building was clearly on the north side of the road, but its exact location and function are not clear. There is no other indication that there was a chapel in this vicinity. Although evidence is slight, the most likely site of the building is what is now No. 27 Yarmouth Road – a site truncated by road-widening in 1956 (see "Between No. 25 Yarmouth Road and School Lane" below). If so, it would have been opposite Nos. 12 and 16 Yarmouth Road. There were cottages on the site by 1800 and nothing by 1841, when it had become the garden of the property adjoining it to the east – part of the Brew Yard estate. It may have been the building called the "Stonehouse" that was acquired by Thomas Vere in 1747, 14 years after he acquired the property on the opposite side of the road (i.e. Nos. 12 and 16 Yarmouth Road).

# Thorpe Hall from 1535

By the early 16th century the hall and parts of the manor estate were let to various tenants. For example, in 1534 the bishop of Norwich let the hall, 84 acres of arable land ("demesne and decayed land") and about 11 acres of meadow to Ralph Cantrell who received 40 shillings a year as keeper of the manor of Thorpe and 20 shillings a year as bailiff of the manor. He paid rent of £7 0s 7d. Although manor courts would continue to have been held at Thorpe Hall, it was principally a farm-house.

A major change to Thorpe Hall happened in the 1590s. Edward Paston had inherited the estate from his father shortly after Edward was born in 1550. Edward married his second wife, Margaret Berney, in the 1580s. In the 1590s he embarked on a series of building campaigns. Brett suggests that he began with Thorpe Hall in about 1590. He then moved on to Binham, where work was abandoned because of a fatal

*Plate 6 : Thorpe Hall from a drawing by T Higham of about 1818.*

accident. In 1596/7, work started on what was to become his principal residence - Appleton Hall, near King's Lynn. In 1612, he built a further hall at Barningham, near Holt.

At Thorpe Hall, Paston remodelled and partly rebuilt the hall. What you can see on the east front of the south wing is largely Paston's work. He made new window openings in the medieval walls, floored the hall and perhaps heightened the building. He also seems to have joined the south and west wings by the addition of a staircase hall. The mainly moulded brick, mullioned and transomed windows with pediments date from this rebuild.

Edward's building work on Thorpe Hall may have been planned as a celebration of his marriage to Margaret Berney. In what may have been the parlour at the north end of the south wing, he inserted a stone fireplace. (In the 1840s this became the dining room). It included the arms of his father, Sir Thomas Paston, impaling the arms of his mother, Ann Leigh, and his own arms impaling those of his wife. The same arms were put on a stone chimney piece in what would have been the hall in the southern half of the south wing. (In the 1840s this became the kitchen).

Edward, a Catholic, turned the house into a cultural centre for the quiet pursuit of music and poetry and built up a large library. It is known from the Norwich Mayor's Court Books that the Earl of Essex's players performed at Thorpe in June 1585. This may have been at Thorpe Hall. It is unlikely that Edward Paston ever resided regularly at Thorpe, though it is clear from his will that he kept a number of books of music in his study there. Correspondence of Lady Katherine Paston of 1603-1627 includes a letter of January 1624 in which Edward wrote that he would go to Thorpe on the first day of the next quarter sessions. He was at Thorpe at the end of May 1624. He had been there at the end of July 1611.

Edward died in 1630 and the property passed to his grandson Clement, also a Catholic. It may have been Clement's principal house. When the Civil War began in 1642, Clement's land was sequestered which meant that all income and profits went to Parliament and its soldiers. The manor was released from sequestration in 1656 and Clement sold it to the Reverend Nathan Wright, a Norwich prebend. A valuation of about 1670 shows that by then the hall had been divided, "the south end of the hall place, the plowman's stable and other houses" having been let to Robert Gimber.

The Manor House (No. 12 Yarmouth Road) dates from the 17th century. It was built outside (but next to) the walled site of Thorpe Hall. In 1733 Thomas Vere purchased it and appears to have lived there. He is important in the history of Thorpe Hall, because, although he purchased the manor of Thorpe in 1751, he does not appear to have moved to Thorpe Hall, but chose to continue to live at the Manor House / Walpole House. Although the names "the Manor House" and "Walpole House" are not recorded until the Harvey sale of 1842, in the enclosure survey of 1800 Thorpe Hall was referred to as "Thorpe Old Hall". This was presumably in contrast with the much more fashionable Manor House / Walpole House. The name "Manor House" may have arisen because Vere lived there while lord of the manor. Vere's fellow MP for Norwich was Horatio Walpole and the name "Walpole House" may have been a tribute to him.

Although the centre of attention had probably moved to the Manor House / Walpole House by say 1730, Thorpe Hall was not neglected. In about 1700 there was some further remodelling. Some rectangular windows were inserted. These can be seen in the west wall of the south wing. It appears from Bardwell's 1760 painting that some outbuildings stood to the east and south of the hall and that between them and the Manor House there was a lane running down to the river. It may have been Thomas Vere who cleared the outbuildings from near the hall and erected replacements further away, including the large barn that is now No. 10A Yarmouth Road. According to notes in the Norfolk Historic Environment Record, the fire that destroyed much of the west wing of the hall happened in the 18th century. No record of this event has been found.

When, in 1806, John Harvey acquired the estate attaching to the manor, he did not choose to live at Thorpe Hall. He was developing his own residence at Thorpe Lodge on the other side of the road. However, he did make some changes to the hall. In particular he probably introduced some Tudor and Jacobean doorways from his family properties in Norwich. This was in line with the growing popularity of antiquarianism. Until about 1970, there was a doorway in the garden entrance to Thorpe Hall, opposite No. 13 Yarmouth Road. In its left-hand spandrel was the merchant mark of Silvester Force, a worsted weaver of St George Colegate. In the other spandrel was the date "1583", which has sometimes mistakenly been regarded as the date of the hall rather than the date of the doorway. Until 1977 there was another doorway on the other side of the road. This was in the octagonal summerhouse opposite No. 2 Yarmouth Road. In the spandrels were the Grocers' arms and the merchant's mark of George Cock, who was mayor in 1613 and lived in Bacon's House, Colegate, from where the door was taken.

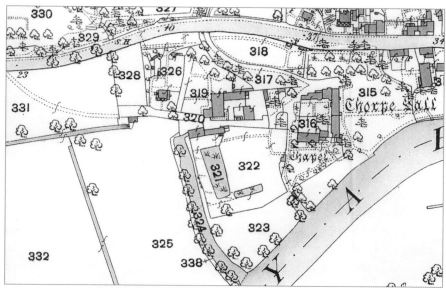

*Plate 7 : Thorpe Hall from the Ordnance Survey 25 inch map of the 1880s.*

There may have been two George Cock doorways at Thorpe Hall. A 17th century doorway was clumsily inserted into the east front of the south wing. It had the initial G in one spandrel and a cock in the other. In addition, there was a door in the short west wing with the date 1608 in a spandrel. According to Ewing, "1608" is the date associated with Cock on a panel and in doorways at Bacon's House.

Comparing the 1800 enclosure map (Plate 4) with the 1825 river map, it seems that between these years, Harvey extended the farm buildings behind the hall, and created a pond garden to the south of them. There were three fishponds in 1825. By 1841 one of them had been filled in. Harvey also dug a second dyke. In addition, he broadened considerably the landing place near the river, taking in the river frontages of what are now Nos. 10 and 14 Yarmouth Road, resulting in a frontage of about 80 yards (73 metres). The purpose may have been to provide a viewing area for spectators at the regatta or "water frolic" that Harvey began in 1821 (see "Thorpe Lodge" above).

In 1838 Harvey gave the hall, with five acres of land, to his sixth daughter, Harriot, who eleven years previously had married Captain Thomas Blakiston, RN. Captain Blakiston was a naval hero and had made a successful and daring escape from France during the Napoleonic Wars. However, according to his brother Peyton, following Captain Blakiston's marriage, his wife "soon acquired a complete command over her husband, and kept him from associating with the other members of his family. They spent much time tracing out the genealogy of the Blakistons in which however they were not very successful."

1838 was the first time that the hall had gone into separate ownership from the farm buildings to the west. In 1841/42, the Blakistons restored, decorated and adapted the hall and grounds for their own use (Plate 7). A new porch was added to the short west wing and a low passage was added to provide access to the west wing. A new main entrance from Yarmouth Road was built - this now leads to No. 4 Yarmouth Road. It bears the arms of Harvey (including three crescents) and

Blakiston (including three cocks). A new drive was constructed from the new entrance to the hall. The old entrance now just led past No. 14 Yarmouth Road. Harvey's extension to the landing place became part of Nos. 10 and 14 Yarmouth Road.

Captain Blakiston died in 1855 and his wife in 1886. Thorpe Hall then passed to Bertha, their youngest daughter, who had married Major Frank Astley Cubitt of Fritton in 1861. He served in the army from 1853 until 1889 and this included service in India at the time of the Indian Rebellion of 1857. Bertha Cubitt died in 1921. Major Cubitt lived into his early nineties and refused to allow any modernisation of the hall, with the result that, on his death in 1929, his son Sir Bertram Cubitt inherited a dilapidated house without electricity, water closets or bathrooms, He could not afford to restore it, and had no choice but to sell.

Initially it was purchased by an antique dealer and then, in 1930, it came into the hands of a boat-builder, Alfred G Ward. He erected two boat-sheds on the riverbank in the southern part of the site. In 1936 the chapel was demolished to make way for an engine repair shop. A few years later, the low extension to the south wing was pulled down. In the 1940s, after the Second World War, No. 4 Yarmouth Road was built. In the 1950s or the 1960s the tall extension at the end of the west wing was demolished. In the early 1960s, Alfred Ward sold his part of the property to Jenners of Thorpe, boat hirers, apart from a site east of the hall where he built a bungalow (No. 8A Yarmouth Road). In the 1960s Jenners built the concrete bridge across the river, south of the hall, as a part of plans to develop a marina complex on the other side of the river. In the early 1970s, Thorpe Hall was sold and the farm buildings were pulled down. They included a farm bungalow north of the principal dyke. In the 1970s vandals set to work on the hall. At the same time, the dining room panelling and stone fireplace surrounds were stolen. Following a campaign, the hall was saved and restored in the 1980s and Thorpe Hall Close was built.

# NUMBERS 10, 10A AND 14 YARMOUTH ROAD

No. 10 Yarmouth Road may date from the late 18th century. It appears to have replaced a coach-house that is referred to in a manor court record. According to this, in 1744, the coach-house was extended northwards seven yards (six metres) beyond what would have been the Thorpe Hall boundary, taking in part of "the waste of the manor". The consequent movement northwards of the road has been referred to above in "Thorpe Hall - Description and history before 1535".

Until the early 1900s there was a pump at the roadside nearly opposite the road that now leads to Thorpe House Langley Preparatory School. The pump was not far from the small garden entrance to Thorpe Hall. It may have been a parish pump, at least for this part of Thorpe.

The pump may have been on a narrow village green that ran along both sides of the road and included the pound that in 1800 was near where the track west of No. 13 Yarmouth Road meets the road, see Plate

*Plate 8 : Yarmouth Road, looking towards Thorpe Narrows, and, on the right, rough ground outside Thorpe Hall with Nos. 10 and 14 Yarmouth Road beyond, in about 1910.*

4 and "Between Thorpe Lodge and No. 25 Yarmouth Road" above. The only surviving remnant of the green is the lay-by outside the old roadside boundary wall of Thorpe Hall (Plate 8). It was encroached upon during the 18th century, and possibly earlier, by the owners of Thorpe Hall moving and rebuilding the boundary wall between the pump and what is now the main entrance to the hall. The site of the building now called No. 10 Yarmouth Road may have previously been part of the green, as it seems to have been the subject of the 1744 licence to enclose "the waste".

Bardwell's 1760 painting suggests that Nos. 14 and 10A Yarmouth Road and the land down to the river were originally part of a lane between outbuildings of Thorpe Hall and the Manor House. Shortly after Bardwell's painting, the lane was closed and No. 10A (a barn) was built across it. Between 1841 and the 1880s No. 14 (Manor Cottage) was built in what had been the yard of the barn.

# NUMBER 25 YARMOUTH ROAD
## FORMERLY THE STORK NURSING HOME AND THE SITE OF THE ORIGINAL GRIFFIN

This is on the opposite side of the road to No. 14 Yarmouth Road. It is an interesting building. Until the Harvey sale in 1842, the site was part of the manor estate. The present main building may encase an earlier building that dates from the late 18th century. By 1725 and until at least 1800 it was the site of the Griffin public house. Bardwell's 1760 painting shows a three-bay building, possibly thatched. In 1800, west of it, was a blacksmith's shop.

The public house had moved to another site by 1825. In 1842, the building on the site was described as "Two Dwelling-Houses, Brick and Tile built, called 'Griffin Cottage'." It can be seen in an 1850 lithograph by J Newman called "Thorpe near Norwich from the railway" (Plate 10).

*Plate 9 : The Gables (now No. 25 Yarmouth Road) and, on the right, Nos. 10 and 14 Yarmouth Road, in about 1905.*

Limestone blocks can be seen in the flint side-wall of the eastern extension of the building. They probably came from the original Griffin or Thorpe Hall.

Between the 1880s and 1907, the main building was either rebuilt or recased (Plate 9). The gables of the new building no longer extended as far as the road and the section between the gables was brought forward. The building was re-roofed and given decorative Tudor-style chimneys. The eastern extension was given a brick façade to the road.

A griffin was the badge of the Pastons who were lords of the manor of Thorpe from 1547 to 1656. Their coat of arms included six fleurs-de-lis. A fleur-de-lis and two griffins (sitting, collared and with wings back to back) can be seen in each of the gables of the building.

As already mentioned, by 1825 the Griffin public house had moved to a site east of asylum (see "St Andrew's Park" below). In 1846 it moved to its present site, west of the asylum.

By the early 20th century, "Griffin Cottage" had become known as "the Gables". It later became the Stork Nursing Home.

It appears from the 1600 Mousehold map (Plate 40) that the eastern boundary of the Griffin was the eastern boundary of "Thorpe several". The several's western boundary was approximately the line of Harvey Lane. "Thorpe several" appears to have been woodland that, following clearance in the 13th or 14th century, was taken into the bishop of Norwich's estate (see "Thorpe Hall - Description and history before 1535" above). By the 16th century it was pasture left open to Mousehold Heath.

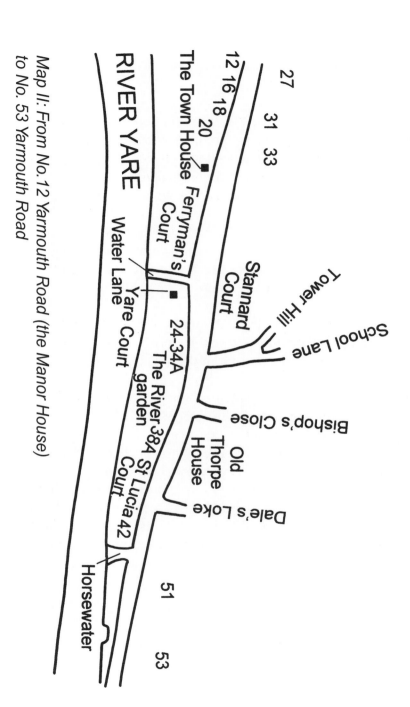

Map II: From No.12 Yarmouth Road (the Manor House) to No. 53 Yarmouth Road

RIVER YARE

12 16 18 20
The Town House
Ferryman's Court
27 31 33
Stannard Court
Tower Hill
School Lane
Water Lane
Yare Court
24-34A
The River 38A
garden
St Lucia 42
Court
Bishop's Close
Old Thorpe House
Dale's Loke
51 53
Horsewater

## II: From No. 12 Yarmouth Road (the Manor House) to No. 53 Yarmouth Road

## NUMBER 12 YARMOUTH ROAD (THE MANOR HOUSE) AND
## NUMBER 16 YARMOUTH ROAD (WALPOLE HOUSE)

On the opposite side of the road to No. 25 and next to No. 14 are the Manor House (No. 12) and Walpole House (No. 16) (Plate 10). The origin of these houses has already been mentioned in "Thorpe Hall – Thorpe Hall from 1535" above.

The Manor House dates from about the middle of the 17th century. Its south façade dates from about 1700. In about 1730 Walpole House was added as a pavilion to the Manor House. In about 1750 the houses began to be treated as separate dwellings. This division did not become permanent until the middle of the 19th century. In the late 18th or early

*Plate 10 : Nos. 25, 10A, 12, 16, 18 and 20 Yarmouth Road from an 1850 lithograph by J Newman.*

19th century, northern additions were made to both houses. The northern addition to the Manor House is now divided between "Well Cottage" and "Manor Lodge".

According to the Norfolk Historic Environment Record, the main east-west block of the Manor House has an external north stack and, in the north wall, blocked large openings on each of the two floor levels, with possible traces of a timber frame. The southern façade of the building is in two sections, one of four bays between rusticated quoins and the other of three bays with a moulded string course.

The original part of Walpole House has three and a half small bell gables protruding above the roof on both its north and south sides, the easternmost of these having been cut in half. They can be seen in Joseph Stannard's *Thorpe Water Frolic – afternoon*, first exhibited in 1825.

South of Walpole House is a garden-house of mid-18th century date, square, with a door, sash window, oriel window and internal stack. The roof is a pyramid. There is internal panelling and a seascape painted over the fireplace.

Two owner-occupiers of the Manor House/Walpole House seem to have been Elizabeth Coulson and Thomas Vere.

Elizabeth Coulson is buried at St Andrew's church, Norwich. She died in 1732 at Thorpe, probably in this house, aged 88. She was the daughter of John Man, mayor of Norwich in 1653 and described as "the richest man in the town". Elizabeth appears to have acquired the property in 1698 and is recorded as living in Thorpe in 1700. She was the older sister of Mary Chapman, who was the wife of Samuel Chapman, rector of Thorpe from 1670 until his death in 1700. It is probable that, following her husband's death, Mary Chapman lived with her sister Elizabeth in this house until Mary died in 1724. Mary is famous as the founder in 1713 of the Bethel Hospital in Norwich. Her memorial stone in Thorpe church records that she built it "wholly at her own expense ...for the reception, maintenance and cure of poor lunaticks". She gave her inheritance from her father, all her income and her estate to the charity she had founded.

On her death in 1732, Elizabeth Coulson bequeathed the Manor House to her granddaughter, Elizabeth Skottow. In the following year, she sold it to Thomas Vere. It was probably at this time that the older part of what is now Walpole House was built as a pavilion to the existing house. Vere, a worsted manufacturer, was mayor of Norwich in 1735. In the same year, he was elected as a Member of Parliament for Norwich, an office he held until 1747. In 1751, Vere purchased the lordship of the manor of Thorpe. In 1755 Vere presented gifts to Thorpe church. According to a note in the parish register, he gave "a set of Silver Communion Plate in a Mahogany Case with Silver Handles, Hinges and Escutcheons, containing Two Flaggons, one Cup, one Waiter, one receiver for the Arms [sic] and a Knife with a Silver Handle. He also erected at his own expense a new Altar-Piece, new floor'd, repaired and painted the seats and beautified" the church. In the same year, he "built a new Schoolroom upon the Town Ground adjoining the Church House" (see "Ferryman's Court" below). In 1766, he died, aged 85. Vere's son, John, does not appear to have lived in Thorpe. He died childless in 1790 and his father's property passed to his father's "much esteemed Friend", Thomas Lobb Chute of South Pickenham.

# NUMBERS 18 AND 20 YARMOUTH ROAD

Structurally, this is one building but originally it was two houses (Plate 10). Its north façade to the street is of seven bays, but the central bay is false, screening the partition wall and central stack.

According to the Norfolk Historic Environment Record, Edmund Cotman, father of the "Norwich School" artist John Sell Cotman, purchased one of the houses (No.18) in 1820, probably when it was newly-built. On 3rd November 1841 John Sell Cotman visited his father there and did a preliminary study for his painting *"From My Father's House at Thorpe"*. It was a modest house of two sitting-rooms, four bedrooms and a kitchen. Edmund Cotman was still living there in 1842 when the freehold was sold in the Harvey sale. At that time Nos. 18 and 20 were referred to as "London House". Edmund Cotman died in 1843.

There is no evidence that John Sell Cotman ever lived in this house or anywhere else in Thorpe. However, according to Moore, his two sons, John Joseph Cotman and Miles Edmund Cotman, also artists, did live in Thorpe between 1849 and 1855. According to the 1851 census, John Joseph Cotman lived close to the Buck (see below), possibly immediately north or north-east of it.

Nos. 18 and 20 Yarmouth Road are now part of the Town House. They were not the first buildings on the site. There was a house there in 1800 and, according to manor court records, had been since at least 1728. A four-bay house is shown in Bardwell's 1760 painting.

# THE TOWN HOUSE

Like the southern façade of the Manor House, this building dates from about 1700 (Plate 11). The Norfolk Historic Environment Record describes it as having "two storeys, the ground floor acting as basement" on the south façade "owing to the slope of the hill".

It goes on to say:

> The north facade is much altered and painted over. The basement windows have been blocked. The south façade has had the ground floor walling removed for a modern extension; the upper level is of five bays in red brick set between rusticated brick quoins... Beyond the east quoins is an extra bay...the brickwork however appears identical. To the east of this are two 20th century additions, infilling a service court, and then another building.... perhaps a stable or coach house.

*Plate 11 : On the left is the Town House from an 1850 lithograph by J Newman.*

There has been much confusion over the name of this building. It was probably called "Town House" not because it was ever a poorhouse or belonged to the parish, but because it adjoined land that both belonged to the parish and was where the Church House (also known as the Town House – see "Ferryman's Court" below) originally stood.

Bardwell's 1760 painting shows it as a five-bay house.

By 1800 it was occupied by Peter Columbine Esq. and was described as "a capital messuage (formerly three tenements)." By 1825 it was occupied by Thomas Davey and by 1886 by George James Newbegin, a Fellow of the Royal Astronomical Society who installed a powerful telescope in the garden. By 1916 the property had passed to Ernest Curl, a department store owner. It was later in the hands of George Jenner, who founded his boating business there.

By the 1950s it had become a hotel. In October 2000 Reginald Kray, a notorious East End gangster, died there.

# BETWEEN NUMBER 25 YARMOUTH ROAD AND SCHOOL LANE

On the other side of the road, between No. 25 Yarmouth Road and School Lane, there is a range of modern buildings that date from the 1960s. The buildings that used to be there were demolished as part of a road-widening scheme in 1956.

Between Nos. 18/20 Yarmouth Road and School Lane a new road was built north of the old one. The old road was closed at both ends and became a service road for the houses on the southern side. Between School Lane and No. 51 Yarmouth Road, Yarmouth Road was widened on its northern side. This involved the demolition of houses at the southern end of School Lane (Plate 14), a reduction in the size of the gardens in front of Thorpe House and No. 51 Yarmouth Road and the demolition of the Guild Cottages that were near the western boundary of No. 51.

This stretch of road had been known as "Thorpe Narrows", because it was only 15 feet (4.5 metres) wide in places, and yet it was part of the main road between Norwich and Yarmouth.

A dramatic consequence of the road widening was the demolition of the buildings between No. 25 Yarmouth Road and School Lane. No. 27 Yarmouth Road (an office building) has been mentioned above in "Thorpe Hall - Description and history before 1535". On the site and in front of what are now No. 29 Yarmouth Road (an office building) and the western quarter of a block of flats called "Conrad Court" (No. 33 Yarmouth Road), there was a group of buildings that in 1842 were referred to as "Brew Yard Estate" (Plate 12). They were opposite what are now Nos. 18/20 Yarmouth Road and the western half of the Town House. In 1842 they consisted of a house, a bakery, seven cottages, a chaise-house, a stable and a large warehouse. Most of the buildings were on the roadside, but the cottages were within Brew Yard. The entry to the yard was opposite where Nos. 18/20 Yarmouth Road joins the Town House. The name "Brew Yard" suggests that there may have been a malt-house here in the late 18th or early 19th century, although no reference to it has been found. The buildings fronting the street were there in 1800.

East of the "Brew Yard Estate" and on the site and in front of most of what is now Conrad Court was another group of buildings. It was opposite what is now the car park east of the Town House and the western end of Ferryman's Court. Near the street were a house and a butcher's shop. Behind them, in 1842, were a barn, stable, cart-lodge, slaughterhouse, piggeries and enclosed yards. Immediately east of these buildings and fronting the street were a house and shop with a plumber's shop at the back. This group of buildings seems to have been erected between 1825 and 1841.

Further east and on the site and in front of what is now Stannard Court (previously a petrol station and shop - No. 39 Yarmouth Road), there were two adjoining houses that, in 1842, were called "Holley Wood". They had shrubberies, a garden, a stable and a chaise-house. The western half of the house was later known as "Hollywood Cottage" and the eastern half "Honeysuckle Cottage". The house was opposite Water Lane. It was there in 1800, when it was owned and occupied by Jeremiah Ives Partridge. Behind this house and the buildings described in the previous paragraph was a chalk and marl pit (see "School Lane and Pinebanks" below).

*Plate 12 : On the left is Brew Yard, just before its demolition in 1956.*

# FERRYMAN'S COURT
## THE SITE OF CHURCH HOUSE AND VERE'S SCHOOL

On the other side of the road to Conrad Court is Ferryman's Court. Although it is a modern development, the land where it stands is of historical interest.

In 1587 the area of land between what is now the Town House and Water Lane (including the car park east of the Town House) was given to the parish by Byrford Lath and Thomas Walker on certain conditions. The land (and any buildings on it) were to be let and the rent applied towards repair of the church and other parish charges. It had a river frontage of 61 yards (56 metres). Until about 1760 the site was commonly known as the Town Land because it belonged to the parish. It was also known as the Rose Ground.

By 1706 the western half of the site was an orchard and in the eastern half, fronting the road, there was a small house. It appears from Bardwell's 1760 painting to have had three bays. It was known as the Town House until 1760, whereupon it became the Church House. The reason for the change of name may have been to distinguish it from the poorhouse that was built in a different part of the parish. The Church House also appears in J Newman's 1850 lithograph "Thorpe near Norwich from the railway" (Plate 13); by then it had been extended.

In 1755 Thomas Vere decided to build a new schoolroom for the parish. It was erected as a western extension to the house mentioned in the previous paragraph. Vere's school replaced an earlier charity school (site unknown) founded in 1700 by the Reverend Samuel Chapman and said in 1709 to be "where 12 poor children were taught to read". In 1839 the Charity Commissioners reported that the schoolmaster at Vere's school taught 12 children in reading and the church catechism and attended with them every Sunday at the church. Two of the scholars were also taught writing. The children were all nominated by the rector. The master was then 70 years of age, and scarcely competent to teach.

He was assisted however by his daughter who kept a "pay school" in a dwelling-house, which he rented. The school remained in use until 1841 when a new school was opened on School Lane. The old school was converted into small houses and so by 1887 the housing on the site was described as "five cottages".

In 1888 the trustees of the Church House sold the land. Shortly afterwards, the cottages were demolished. In the 1950s the site was occupied by Jenners' boat-sheds. It is now occupied by modern flats - Ferryman's Court - and a car park.

From the 1861 census, it appears that "Thorpe Street" was the part of Yarmouth Road between the cottages on the site of Ferryman's Court and Thunder Lane.

# WATER LANE

It has been established that this is a public right of way (Plate 13). In 1587 it was referred to as a common lane. In 1716 it was known as Watering Lane or Water Lane. Since 1767 it has been known simply as Water Lane. "Watering Lane" suggests it was a place where animals, particularly horses, were brought to drink (see also "Horsewater and the Watering Place" below). The 1841 tithe map describes it as a "landing place" i.e. a place where goods were landed from the river. Water Lane now runs under the western end of Yare Court.

*Plate 13 : On the left is the Church House and then Water Lane from an 1850 lithograph by J Newman.*

# BETWEEN WATER LANE AND THE RIVERGARDEN
## (FORMERLY THE KING'S HEAD)

Between Water Lane and the Rivergarden are:
(1) modern flats (Yare Court) and a pair of Edwardian semi-detached houses (Nos. 24 and 26 Yarmouth Road),
(2) two large Victorian houses (Nos. 28 and 30 Yarmouth Road) and
(3) a smaller Victorian building and a 1930s (?) engineering works (Nos. 32, 34 and 34A Yarmouth Road).

From at least the mid-18th century these were three separate tenements. Where the western extension to No. 28 Yarmouth Road now is used to be part of the first tenement. Bardwell's 1760 painting shows a row of probably three cottages in the middle of the site.

In 1829 the tenements were briefly united when a large house was built on what was the second tenement and its gardens extended across the other two tenements. In 1842 it was described as a "capital Dwelling-house". It had a "large walled-in Garden, between the house and the river, with a terrace walk of fifty yards (46 metres) next the latter". There was also a stable and chaise-house and a gardener's cottage. By 1842 the cottage had been converted into a laundry. However, by the 1880s the house and garden had gone and there were three separate tenements again.

# SCHOOL LANE AND PINEBANKS

On the other side of the road is School Lane.

The cottages on the right appear from the date-stone to have been built in 1867 by Donald Dalrymple who was then living at Thorpe Lodge. The cottages replaced a cottage, blacksmith's shop and warehouse that were here by 1841. When Yarmouth Road was widened in 1956, the first of the cottages, No. 1 School Lane, was demolished, as was No. 45 Yarmouth Road that adjoined it (Plate 14).

Beyond the cottages is an old school. The original school was built in 1841 and consisted of a large room 40 feet (12 metres) by 12 feet (3.5 metres) with a door, into the lane, at the west end. The basis of this large room can be seen in the centre of the present building. An incised tablet lists the names of the original subscribers and trustees. In 1855 the school was enlarged and in 1872 a large schoolroom was added. An infants' school, with its own entrance, was added in 1899. The buildings continued in use as schools until they were superseded

*Plate 14 : On the left are Nos. 45, 47 and 49 Yarmouth Road and the garden wall of Thorpe House, just before they were demolished in 1956.*

by new schools in Hillside Avenue, in 1937, and St William's Way, in 1952.

School Lane originated as a north-south path between what is now Yarmouth Road and what was, until 1801, Yarmouth Way. It was a path between the river and Mousehold Heath. Until it was diverted in 1953, School Lane met what had been Yarmouth Way near where buildings now stand in the north-west corner of a playing field just south of Henby Way. Part of the present School Lane runs southwards from White Farm Lane to Pinebanks. If this continued southwards as far as the end of the Pinebanks buildings, it seems from the 1600 Mousehold map (Plate 40) that it would equate with a lane that ran between "Thorpe several" to the west (see "No. 25 Yarmouth Road" above) and "Thorpe Closes" to the east.

From School Lane to about 100 yards (91 metres) east of South Avenue, there is an accessible band of chalk running about 50 yards (46 metres) northwards from Yarmouth Road. There have been chalk and marl pits here since at least the early 18th century. In the Rye Manuscripts at the Norfolk Record Office, there is a Counsel's Opinion of 1757 advising that marl and lime chalk had been dug in this part of Thorpe "for a great length of time". Evidence of pits can be seen on the western side of Tower Hill, between Tower Hill and School Lane, at the top of Chapel Lane, and a short distance east of South Avenue. The Tower Hill / School Lane pit appears to have been started in the 1920s and extended after the Second World War. However, the 1800 enclosure map (Plate 44) shows that the South Avenue pit dates from at least the 18th century. A 1697 deed shows that the Chapel Lane pit dates from at least the 17th century.

According to Marshall and Young, in the late 18th century, white marl was being transported by river from Thorpe to Woodbastwick, Ludham, Thrigby, Hembsy, and Langley. It was laid on the land to improve its productivity. At Langley, they laid 12 loads per acre at 4s 6d a load from the keel or barge. Tower Hill may have developed as a way into the pit. (In the 1861 census it was referred to as Marl Pit Lane). The pit between Tower Hill and School Lane is a pit within a pit or quarry. The same has happened with the pit at the end of Chapel Lane.

From 1953 until 2008, School Lane led to Pinebanks (No. 9 Yarmouth Road). This was Norwich Union's (later Aviva's) sports and leisure centre. The building dates from about 1880 and was built by John Odin Howard Taylor. He was a Norwich solicitor, a minor poet and a famous chess player. The house was known as Pine Banks Tower, because of the brick and flint tower that was built next to it. According to Rye, it was also known as "Taylor's Folly".

In 1883 the tower was used for a charity chess tournament. In 1887 Queen Kapiolani of Hawaii visited it. She was in Britain to attend the celebration of Queen Victoria's Golden Jubilee. An inscription on the tower reads: "HM Kapiolani ascended this tower June 6th 1887. Quis enim." On the other side of the tower is a quotation from Horace "Omne tulit punctum qui miscuit utile et dulci" which translates as "He has gained every point who has mixed the useful with the sweet".

In 1890 Taylor died and Pinebanks passed through various hands. In 1919 Thomas Jarrold bought it and in 1953 Norwich Union purchased it. In 2008 Aviva closed it. It was then sold. It is in the process of being redeveloped for housing. It is expected that the Pinebanks house and tower will remain.

# THE RIVERGARDEN
## FORMERLY THE KING'S HEAD

On the other side of the road is the Rivergarden (Plates 14 and 15). The earliest part of the present buildings may date from the 17th century. It is L-shaped and is in the north-west quarter of the plot. It is of flint and brick and has a steep-pitched, hipped roof. There are three arched windows facing the road. It returns along the western edge of the plot with a shaped gable towards the river. All the other older buildings appear to be 19th century. The northern end of the 17th century building seems to have been "recased" at the same time.

The 1800 enclosure map indicates that at that time there were what were probably outbuildings in the north-east quarter of the plot, bordering what may have been a stable yard. They may have included the steep-pitched rubble and pantile eastern extension of the present buildings. The end of this extension marks what was the eastern extent of the plot.

There was an open space, probably a lawn or bowling green, in the southern half of the plot. A pencil drawing of 1806 by John Crome - *View from the King's Head Gardens at Thorpe* (see Clifford, Plate 73) - shows several men sitting or standing under a covered arbour or box on the western side of the lawn.

By 1841 all the buildings in the north-east quarter of the plot (apart from the eastern extension referred to above) had gone and most of the 19th century additions had been made. This meant that, from the roadside, the King's Head looked much as it does today. One difference was that at the end of the eastern extension, there was another building that ran down to the river. This may have been the covered arbour on the eastern side of the lawn that can be seen in an 1850 lithograph (Plate 15).

The fall in the ground means that what are single-storey buildings from the roadside are two-storey buildings from the south. The south front has been much altered.

The building was known as the King's Head from at least 1700, when John Bunting is recorded as living there. In 1767 the land from Water Lane up to and including the King's Head was in same ownership, although with different tenants. This was still the case in 1825 but had changed by 1841. In April 2000 the name of the King's Head was changed to the Rivergarden.

*Plate 15 : The King's Head from an 1850 lithograph by J Newman.*

# OLD THORPE HOUSE
## FORMERLY THORPE HOUSE

On the other side of the road is "Old Thorpe House". This dates from the late 17th century. The section of this date is at the front of the building. The building was extended northwards in about 1730. Evidence of this comes from a brick dated 1732. At the same time as this extension, the southern façade of the house was altered. Western and eastern extensions were added to the house between 1825 and 1841. When the building was surveyed in 1962, some late 17th century panelling remained and there was a portion of 18th century stair-rail in the attic. In the oldest part of the house were some ovolo-moulded beams. The house has incorporated earlier doorways. There used to be a grand 16th century doorway with a four-centred arch and deeply-carved panels depicting leaves, fruit and fish between curving folds. In 1993 the house included a fine Jacobean door with figures on one side and a coat of arms on the other, bearing a faint name that seemed to be Ballantyne. Most of the 19th century additions to the building have now gone, apart from the western extension to the main house.

Old Thorpe House is between Bishop's Close to the west and Dale's Loke to the east. What is now the northern half of Bishop's Close used to be a continuation of Dale's Loke. In 1741 the manor court said that the then owner of the house, William Payne, could block an ancient footway running up the west side of his property from what is now Yarmouth Road up to what was, until 1801, Yarmouth Way. There was a condition. He was required to make a new footway up to the said way on the east side of his house. This suggests that Dale's Loke originated as an 18th century track up to Yarmouth Way, but, before 1741, it ran up the west rather than the east side of the house. The 1800 enclosure map shows a section of this path (west of Thompson's Folly) as a roadway. This supports the idea that the footpath represented an important division between woodland to the west and arable fields to the east (see "Thorpe Hall - Description and history before 1535" above and "The original church and settlement" and Plate 42 below).

From about 1840 until his death in 1864, Charles Weston, a Norwich brewer, owned Thorpe House. From 1897 until the early 1950s, it was run as private school. Until 1946 it was known as Thorpe High School. It then became Thorpe House School.  In the early 1950s, the school moved to a house that was originally called "Sunny Hill" – south-west of Pinebanks. The school came to an end in 2010 (see "Between Thorpe Lodge and No. 25 Yarmouth Road" above).

In 1841 Grigor noted that at the edge of the river opposite Thorpe House, there was "a celebrated tree of the white willow, of magnitude sufficient to have induced some person to take advantage of it in building a shed, of which it forms an end. This tree is well-known to all the villagers, and they reckon no picture of Thorpe complete without it."

*Plate 16 : View across the river to a foundry (now No.38A Yarmouth Road) in about 1910.*

# NUMBER 38A YARMOUTH ROAD
## THE SITE OF A FOUNDRY

On the other side of the road, after the Rivergarden, is No. 38A Yarmouth Road. Historically, the plot where it stands ran from the end of the eastward extension of the Rivergarden to the end of the 19th century building that is now No. 38A Yarmouth Road.

Now, the western half of the plot does not contain any buildings. However, by 1841 there were cottages along both the eastern and western halves of the street frontage with a staithe behind. By the 1880s there were buildings behind as well as on the street frontage. On the western side of the plot was a single-storey building running down to the river. On the eastern side of the plot there were smaller buildings and a yard that was entered through what is now the garage of 38A Yarmouth Road. Together these buildings formed a foundry that had been built in the 1860s (Plate 16). An 1868 directory refers to the occupier, Thomas Sabberton, as an "engineer, iron and brass founder, boiler maker and general smith and coal merchant". This was the same Thomas Sabberton who had previously been a blacksmith in School Lane. The foundry was still operating in 1907 but had been demolished by 1926. In 1954 No. 38A Yarmouth Road became Foundry House and in 1961 Foundry House Hotel. In 1961 the hotel amalgamated with the Santa Lucia Hotel and a new building (since demolished) was erected behind it, near the river.

# NUMBERS 1-4 ST LUCIA COURT
## FORMERLY SANTA LUCIA HOTEL AND THE SITE OF THE MAID'S HEAD

The four-gabled building that is now Nos. 1-4 St Lucia Court was until 1994 the Santa Lucia Hotel. It was built between 1864 and 1871, as part of a complete redevelopment of the site. In 1881 it was referred to as "The Villa" and in 1901 as "Shamrock Villa".

Before it was redeveloped, the plot had been 23½ yards (21.5 metres) wide on the riverside and had been divided by a track that went down to the river as a continuation of what is now Dale's Loke. There were cottages on either side of the track as well as a cottage on the roadside. The cottage on the west side of the track appears to have been a building that in 1800 was described as the Maid's Head public house. It appears in a painting of c.1814-1817 by John Thirtle called *Cottage by the River at Thorpe, Norwich* (Plate 17 – see also Allthorpe-Guyton, Plate 4b, No. 42). By 1841 the building had been demolished, although the cottages on the roadside and on the east side of the track remained until the 1864/1871 redevelopment.

(Norwich Castle Museum & Art Gallery)

*Plate 17 : "Cottage by the River at Thorpe, Norwich" by John Thirtle, between 1814 and 1817, showing the way up from the river past the Maid's Head public house, in the foreground, and, in the distance, Thorpe House.*

# NUMBER 42 YARMOUTH ROAD
## POINT HOUSE

This building was being constructed in 1864 when it was referred to as "The River Side Villa Residence (at present unfinished)". It had been owned by Charles Weston (see "Old Thorpe House" above). Following his death, his properties were sold by auction and are listed in the Norfolk Chronicle of 30th July 1864. When Point House was built, it replaced a double-gabled cottage on the riverside and a cottage that faced what is now Horsewater. The riverside cottage was a popular subject for artists of the Norwich School. John Thirtle's painting *Old Waterside Cottages* dates from c.1814-1817 (see Rajnai). John Crome's *On the Yare* has been dated to c.1812-1814 (see Clifford, Plate 121a).

# NUMBER 51 YARMOUTH ROAD
## GUILD HOUSE

On the other side of the road is 51 Yarmouth Road. The house dates from the late 18th century. In 1800 it was owned and occupied by Ann Sayer. From at least 1845 (White's Norfolk Directory), it has been known as the Guild House. The Norfolk Historic Environment Record refers to its "pedimented doorway between two unequally projecting wings with bay windows and modillion eaves cornice". It is of brick with a slate and pantile roof.

Near its western boundary were the Guild Cottages. They were demolished by road-widening in 1956 (see " Between No. 25 Yarmouth Road and School Lane" above).

# HORSEWATER AND THE WATERING PLACE

Opposite No. 51 Yarmouth Road is "Horsewater". This was the western edge of the village green (see "River Green" below). Until about 1800, the green stretched unenclosed from here eastwards to what was the edge of the Tuns (now the wall of the public toilets near the Rushcutters). Almost all of the green was regarded as a place where copyhold tenants of the manor had the right to water their horses and cattle. A survey of 1767 divided the green into three sections from west to east. First there were 276 yards (252 metres) of "The Watering Place", then 19½ yards (18 metres) of Town Land and then a further 35 yards (32 metres) of "The Watering Place".

By the early 19th century the right to water horses and cattle was being associated with particular areas of the green. There were two watering places. The first was where Horsewater is now. The second was a few yards further east opposite what is now the boundary between Nos. 51 and 53 Yarmouth Road. The first of these is shown somewhat imaginatively in John Joseph Cotman's *Thorpe Watering*, painted in 1875, but based on earlier depictions of the scene - see Walpole page 101. The second is shown in John Thirtle's "*Thorpe Watering*" - see Allthorpe-Guyton, Plate 42, No. 79.

Continued use of the watering places led to the crumbling away of the road so that both the road and waterings became unsafe. A horse was carried away by the river and drowned. As already mentioned, opposite the waterings was 51 Yarmouth Road. In about 1830, Henry Leathes acquired it, enclosed the land opposite the house and next to Horsewater and began improving it. Leathes and the next owner of No. 51 (H S Patteson) spent at least £100 each raising the road and the riverbank, carting a large quantity of the soil for that purpose and constructing a quay-heading to protect the road (see Eastern Daily Press 16th April 1879).

In 1836 Henry Leathes was granted a license to enclose. The second watering is gone and the area remains enclosed with a boathouse and an area of private moorings. Further east, opposite No. 53 Yarmouth Road, the green is also enclosed and has been since at least the 1880s. This is presumably for reasons of safety, as the land is narrow and steep here.

# NUMBER 53 YARMOUTH ROAD
## ST ANDREW'S COURT FORMERLY THE RECTORY

On the other side of the road is No. 53 Yarmouth Road. This was built in the 1860s as a rectory, following the acquisition of the land by the church in December 1863. William Birkbeck granted the church the land and 18 acres of marsh and meadow in exchange for the former rectory (No. 103 Yarmouth Road) and 16 acres of glebe land behind it. The new rectory was built at the same time as the present church (1864-1866). They were planned together. A track that used to run along the western boundary of the old churchyard was incorporated into the grounds of the new rectory. The track was no longer necessary because the new church was built on the site of the buildings the track had previously led to. The house continued in use as the rectory until 1959.

In the 1860s an existing house was demolished to make way for the rectory. The house can be seen in an early photograph (see Supple, opposite page 30). It shows what may be a four-bay, three-storey house with a single-storey western extension. Grigor mentions the garden in 1841 when he refers to "several large trees of the cluster pine (*Pinus Pinaster*), in the garden of the Reverend W Frost". In 1800 it was referred to as a "Mansion House" and had 5 acres of garden and plantation. It is clear from manor court records that it was built by Robert Baret of Norwich between 1757 and 1773 on the site of a bakery. This may be the "Robert Barett" who was a sheriff of Norwich in 1765. It seems likely that until the 16th century the area taken up by the old church and churchyard used to be part of this tenement - see "The old church and the movement of the settlement" below.

In 1781 Armstrong described Thorpe as "delightfully situated on a hanging hill", and having "become of late the residence of opulent manufacturers, several of whom have erected extensive buildings in it, and laid out spacious gardens". He continued that the "village of Thorpe is sometimes called the Richmond of Norfolk, and may vie with the proudest and most admired summer retreats in all England."

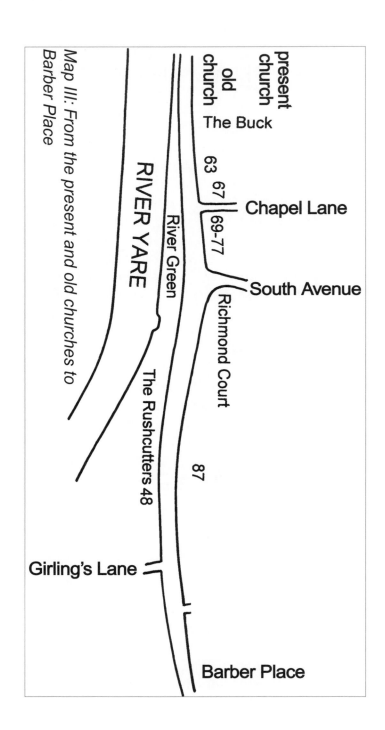

Map III: From the present and old churches to Barber Place

# III: From the present and old churches to Barber Place

## THE PRESENT CHURCH

Next to No. 53 Yarmouth Road (and linked to it by an entry through the boundary wall) is the present parish church of St Andrew (Plate 20). This replaced the old church, the tower of which can be seen in front of it.

According to Supple (pages 108-9), in "May 1862 it was resolved that additional accommodation be provided in the Church, and that no rate be struck, but subscriptions invited. The immediate response was a sum of £520." Two years later, in 1864, it was decided that enlarging the existing, small building was impracticable. To have done so, it would have been necessary to destroy much of the original fabric. Instead, a new church would be built behind the old church, on a site given by William Birkbeck. Work began in the same year.

The reason given for having a new church was to have an "edifice more adapted to the requirements of the increasing population of the village". Between 1801 and 1851 the population of Thorpe Hamlet (the part of Thorpe west of Harvey Lane) had increased rapidly from 74 to 1,811 and so in 1852 a church (St Matthew's) had been built there and the area had become a separate ecclesiastical district. Between 1801 and 1861 the population of the rest of Thorpe (to the east of Harvey Lane) had increased steadily from 335 to 1,072. At the 1851 Religious Census the old church had 267 sittings. The new church was designed to seat "more than 500".

The architect for the new church was Thomas Jeckyll (1827-81). He had been responsible for a number of slightly odd churches, including Holt Methodist Church (1862-3). The church consists of nave, chancel and south aisle, both the chancel and the aisle ending in an apse. The arrangement was such that, in the words of a Norfolk Chronicle reporter in 1866, "should the building be found too small for the congregation, which its expected improved arrangements will increase, another aisle could be added on the north side without materially interfering with other parts of the structure".

The church is 117 feet (35.5 metres) long and 48 feet (14.5 metres) wide. It is in the "plate tracery" style of the 13th century with elements of Decorated and Transitional. The exterior of the building is of flint, the dressings being of white sandstone, and the roof is of small red square tiles. The reporter referred to above described the outer walls as "exhibiting far too much of that 'station' style of architecture which, in so many instances, at the present day, marks the eccentricities rather than the taste of the designer".

He preferred the interior walls of the new church. They were of warm red brick, relieved by "neat fillets of white brick and squared flint." The walls are now painted over. The nave is divided from the south aisle by five arches of brick and white stone. The pillars carrying the arches are of red Mansfield marble with Roche Abbey stone capitals. At the time of the consecration in May 1866, the capitals had been left in their rough state, "the state of the funds not allowing them to be richly carved in foliage as they are designed to be". Stone carving around doorways was left undone. There was also no tower. This was because by 1866 only 75% of the necessary funds (£4,000) had been raised.

The stone carving was probably completed by 1881. Now the most curious feature of the church is the aisle arcade. Pevsner described the "short round piers on high bases with square capitals and abaci, i.e. Transitional, but with colossal capitals, with some semi-Norman motifs but also a pelican and busts of angels."

As well as providing the site, William Birkbeck provided a large proportion of the funds for the new church. Birkbeck was a banker, a shrewd businessman and a benefactor. He was a leading figure in the life of the parish from about 1858 until his death in 1897. He probably saw himself as the successor to John Harvey (see "Thorpe Lodge" above) who was said by the Norwich Mercury in 1866 to "have established the modern prosperity of the village". In 1871 Birkbeck employed Thomas Jeckyll to design a large extension and make other alterations to High House (No. 91 Thunder Lane - see "South Avenue etc" below).

An unusual feature of the new church was that, viewed from the road, it was somewhat hidden by the old church. It was intended to let the old church "fall into decay, when a better view of the new will be obtained through the ruins." It did not decay very quickly.

In 1881 a faculty was obtained "to dilapidate the old church and chancel". In 1882 the old church was converted into a "picturesque ruin" and a long porch with a tower and spire over it (150 feet or 45.5 metres high) was added to the new church. Bells were added in 1883. In 1944 a landmine explosion cracked the spire and in 1956 a much shorter spire (30 feet or 9 metres high) replaced it.

During the 20th century, changes to the church included a new organ in 1901 and, in 1920, a chancel screen that was erected as a memorial to the dead of the First World War. The artist, Mr A Kingston Rudd of Sandringham, provided the twelve apostles with portrait heads. In the Eastern Evening News of 14th May 1957, many years after the artist had died, it was disclosed that the portraits were, from left to right:

St Thomas - Admiral Michael de Ruyter,
St James the Less - from Rubens' 'Adoration of the Magi',
St Bartholomew - Miss Mabel Jacobs,
St Simon - General Sir Dighton Probyn VC,
St John - an American actress (name forgotten by artist),
St Andrew - Bishop King of Lincoln,
St Peter - Lord Salisbury,
St James the Great - Mr Philip Rice of Wolferton,
St Jude - Charles I,
St Matthew - the Reverend Henry ffolkes of Hillington,
St Philip - Lord Leighton and
St Matthias - Bishop King of Lincoln in extreme old age.

# THE OLD CHURCH AND THE MOVEMENT OF THE SETTLEMENT

Much of the old church is now in ruins. However, the tower over the south porch remains fully intact. The south and west walls of the nave survive to a substantial extent. The old church was built of coursed flint, brick and limestone. Little remains of the chancel. A spur of masonry shows the line of the chancel south wall. The south respond of the chancel arch is also intact and built of chamfered Tudor brick. Bryant quotes Mackerell who, writing in 1744, said that the old church was 25 yards (23 metres) long and 7 yards (6 metres) wide and had no aisles (Plate 18). There was a square tower over the south porch with two bells. The tower was no taller than the ridge of the church roof. The nave roof was thatched and the chancel roof tiled. Inside, the altar was raised on two steps and railed in. On the chancel screen were what appear to have been 14th century coats of arms of the Folliot and Hastings families of Elsing, near East Dereham. There was also an octagonal font of the 15th or 16th century. In addition, there were various memorial stones of the 17th or 18th century, the earliest with a date, according to Mackerell, being 1644. (Norris, writing in the early 1730s, identified a stone dated 1616). Several stones were unidentifiable, having been robbed of their brasses. The most intriguing was an indented stone showing the outline of an armed figure with a lion or dog at his feet and a cushion under his head.

Norris mentioned a "Helmet and two Irons for Pennons" at the east end of the chancel. He speculated that they could have been for Sir Thomas Paston, lord of the manor of Thorpe, who died in 1550. However, he is known to have been buried at Appleton, near King's Lynn.

In 1815 a small gallery was built at the west end of the nave, approached by a stone staircase in the tower. Schoolchildren used to sit in the gallery.

When the old church was turned into a ruin, many of the monuments from that church were transferred to the long porch of the new church. Having been lost for many years, the font from the old church was discovered and moved into the new church.

The 1864/1866 building of the new church and rectory included changes to the churchyard. Up until then the Buck had been the eastern boundary of the churchyard. The north-west corner of the Buck had marked the line of the churchyard's northern boundary, which curved slightly southwards to the present curve in the wall immediately south of the access between the present church and No. 53 Yarmouth Road. Between that boundary and the property to the north, there was a yard that widened towards the east. In the 19th century the yard seems to have contained a cottage and what were probably outbuildings. It was reached by a track that ran between the western boundary of the churchyard and the eastern boundary of the adjoining property.

*Plate 18 : The old church and part of the Buck in about 1860.*

This yard and track disappeared when space was cleared for the building of the present church and No. 53 Yarmouth Road (then the new rectory). However, their unusual nature suggests that the church was "planted" on part of an existing tenement, which seems from the 1800 enclosure map to have been what is now No. 53 Yarmouth Road. This adds weight to the theory that the old church was not Thorpe's original church, but that it was moved to its present site between 1500 and 1550, having previously been located at the top of the Hillside Avenue allotments (see "The original church and settlement" below).

The theory was first put forward by Rose and Davison in 1988. It means that the old church was built not earlier than the beginning of the 16th century and that any older features it contained (i.e. the font, if it does predate the old church, and the screen) were brought down from the original church.

A strong argument for the theory is the liberal use of Tudor brick, for example in the tower. Batcock noted that the tower is constructed of flint but there is a lot of brick. The put-log holes (for scaffolding) are lined with brick. Up to 13 feet (4 metres) from the ground (i.e. about the top of porch level) the quoins are of limestone. Above that, they are of brick. Although this suggests a building break, the use of brick in the arches of the openings above and below the "break" indicates a single phase.

Batcock suggested that the tower resembled a domestic entrance porch of the Tudor period rather than a church tower. He concluded that the tower and the rest of the old church were of one principal phase, and the abundant use of Tudor brick suggested a date in the first half of the 16th century.

Why was the church moved? It is quite likely that this happened in connection with a shift in the focus of settlement from the top of the Hillside Avenue allotments to the river. This may have been linked with a growing importance of river trade and possibly mineral extraction. It may also be linked with the conversion from arable to pasture which seems to have affected the area between Harvey Lane and Thunder Lane in the 15th or 16th century (see "The original church and settlement" and Plate 42 below).

Between Thorpe Hall and the Rushcutters, there is direct access to the river from the gravel terrace and so this was an obvious settlement site, although somewhat cramped by the rising ground to the north. The 1600 Mousehold map (Plate 40) shows Thorpe Hall and the Rushcutters with the church in a central position along this riverside strip. There are three buildings on either side of the church. The building immediately east of the church is likely to be the Buck. It dates from about 1600. Then there is No. 63 Yarmouth Road that has a date-stone of 1586. The next building is probably the cottages that stood on the site of what is now No. 67 Yarmouth Road. It seems from the 1800 enclosure map that the buildings from the church to the No. 67 Yarmouth Road cottages formed a distinct block of development (Plate 19).

*Plate 19 : The area near the old church from the 1800 enclosure map, showing the track that went round the church. 85 is the Buck, 84 is No.63 and 83 is No.67.*

The Rushcutters is also likely to date from about 1600. This suggests that many new buildings were being erected during the 1580s and 1590s, at least 30 or 40 years after the suggested date for the old church. In 1587, some land between the road and the river was given to the church to provide income that could be used towards church repairs (see "Ferryman's Court" above). Repair was needed by 1597, when at the bishop's visitation, it was reported that the church roof needed thatching, which, in itself, suggests the church must have been built at least 30 or 40 years earlier.

One change that took place between 1461 and 1556 was the building of a new road from Norwich to Thorpe. This included what is now Rosary Road, part of Thorpe Road and Yarmouth Road up to just beyond the railway bridge, where it joined Yarmouth Way (see "Nos. 205 and 207 Yarmouth Road etc" below). The only part of it that may have been completely new was the part between Thunder Lane and the railway bridge. This is because it cut through the existing common field. The rest was probably a development of existing tracks or paths between woodland and meadow or rising ground and the river.

A draft Norwich charter of 1461 describes the eastern boundaries of the city in some detail for the first time. It refers to boundary cross that stood in "a certain way below a wood called Thorpe Wood which leads from Norwich to Postwick above a hill called Leonard's Hill." The reference to "Leonard's Hill" and the way "from Norwich to Postwick" suggests that this was Yarmouth Way. It ran up Gas Hill, then eastwards along the southern boundary of Mousehold Heath, which included the northern boundary of the wood west of Harvey Lane (which a draft charter of 1461 and the Norwich charter of 1556 referred to as Thorpe Wood). It then continued eastwards from Rockland Drive to just east of Hilly Plantation, then south-eastwards to just after where the railway bridge crosses Yarmouth Road and then eastwards to Postwick (Plates 42 and 43). A new charter of 1556 refers instead "to the high way leading from our said City of Norwich to the vill of Thorpe", which suggests that by this time the new road to Thorpe had been built. Where it joined Yarmouth Way can be seen on the 1589 Mousehold map. It appears to have been a private road belonging to "Mr Gybson". He may be the same person as Thomas Gibson esquire of Thorpe whose will was proved in 1616 and who is the earliest recorded owner of what is now the Rushcutters (see "the Rushcutters" below). The same map shows "the olde Churche pathe" leading from the heath across Yarmouth Way to the original church (see also "No. 127 Yarmouth Road etc" below).

The "moving" of the church, the replanting of the village and the building of a new road suggests the influence of important men. Goreham has suggested the influence of the Pastons, who were lords of the manor of Thorpe from 1547. Although this is certainly possible, there is no evidence of them spending money in Thorpe until the late 16th century when Edward Paston rebuilt Thorpe Hall. More likely candidates are the Howards who feature in the history of Thorpe in the 1540s. Their heraldic badge, the White Lion, was the former name of the Buck, the public house immediately to the east of the old church.

In 1542 Henry Howard, Earl of Surrey, obtained a lease of St Leonard's Priory (on the top of Gas Hill), where he began building a great house that became known as Mount Surrey. In 1544 the Howards were granted the lordship of the manor of Thorpe. In 1545 Surrey obtained a lease of "the partible woode of Thorp". Two years later, in 1547, Surrey was executed for treason.

As far as the old church is concerned, it is very unlikely that Surrey acted on his own. In 1535 the bishop of Norwich had granted Thomas Godsalve, his registrar, the patronage of Thorpe church. Godsalve was, according to MacCulloch, "one of a family with close ties" to the Howards. A 1552 inventory of church goods lists simply a bell and "one cope of green say". There is no mention of any communion plate. This would suggest that the church was very poor and had needed to sell most of its goods to raise enough money to comply with new legislation. It is possible that some of the goods had been sold to finance the building of the old church.

One factor that may have been a catalyst for the changes that happened in the 16th century was the forced departure, in 1535, of the bishop of Norwich as the lord of the manor and principal landowner. The lands were seized by Henry VIII, who held them until 1544. This release from episcopal control may have created the right conditions for the changes.

# RIVER GREEN AND ITS MANY USES
## (INCLUDING AS THE SITE OF THE FIRST POORHOUSE)

On the other side of the road is River Green (Plate 20).

As mentioned already, the green was a watering place for horses and cattle (see "Horsewater and the Watering Place" above). Until about 1800, it stretched unenclosed from Horsewater to what was the edge of the Tuns (now the wall of the public toilets near the Rushcutters). As well as a watering place, the green was also a common staithe, where goods could be loaded and unloaded from vessels.

In 1757 the owners of the houses facing the green claimed this right. They said that for a great length of time they had unloaded and loaded keels and lighters there and had erected a staithe. At that time the loads would have included large quantities of marl and lime chalk that had been dug from the Thorpe pits. For example, it is clear from 18th century manor court rolls that the tenants of the Buck had rights over the 25 yards (23 metres) of common staithe opposite their premises. The tenants of the limekiln immediately north of the Buck also had rights over this part of the staithe and this included rights to "leave and lay" on the staithe "stones, gravel, lime, sand and chalk" from the kiln.

It is clear from material in the Rye Manuscripts that by 1766 rights over the green extended to all copyhold tenants of the manor. A tenant claimed they had the right to dig pits and fell top wood. This was not challenged. By 1766 the parish, which owned the land where the parish staithe now is, were claiming rights over the green. This is why, at about that time, they erected a parish staithe and enclosed it with iron railings. It may have been on the same site as the staithe that was erected in 1844 at the end of the green between where the present public staithe is and the wall of the toilet block. The intention may have been that this staithe should supersede the common staithe rights. It continued in use during the 19th century.

*Plate 20 : View across the river and the green to No.53 Yarmouth Road, the present and old churches, the Buck and the buildings immediately west of No.63 Yarmouth Road, in about 1905.*

From an unknown date until 1769, the village poorhouse (or town house) "stood by the riverside" between "the Road and the Common River about 100 yards (91 metres) from the Church". This suggests it stood on the green opposite Chapel Lane, not far from where the war memorial now stands. However, it is more likely that it was on the site of what is now the public staithe, since this was land that belonged to the parish. The town house was described as a cottage that was divided into three tenements.

In 1776 village stocks were acquired from Postwick and set up on the green opposite the church. They are depicted in James Stark's "*View on the Yare, near Thorpe Church*", published in 1829. According to Supple (page 95), the stocks were there until 1852.

The 1841 tithe map shows a parish lock-up, known as "The Cage", standing by the riverside on what is now the public staithe, opposite what is now Richmond Court. Before a regular police force began in 1840s, the parish constable was responsible for the village stocks and lock-up. A lock-up was a gaol where felons were detained pending their removal to court and drunks and troublemakers were locked up for the night. Supple (page 95) quotes someone who remembered it as "a sort of box" that "was erected to save taking a prisoner up to Norwich at a late hour." He believed "only one prisoner was ever put in it – probably for drunkenness – and when he awoke next morning, not knowing where on earth he was, he nearly, as they say, 'went off his head'. "

Thirtle's *Thorpe St Andrew* (see Allthorpe-Guyton, Plate 40, No. 80) and John Crome's *View on the Yare* (see Clifford, Plate 121a) show a small building by the riverside towards the Rushcutters. It also appears on the 1800 enclosure map. It belonged to the parish, but it is not clear what it was. It has been suggested that it was where the water-cart was kept that was used for laying dust on the road.

Vestry minutes show that the lock-up referred to above was not erected until 1834. By the 1880s it had gone and a group of trees had been planted in its place. The Ordnance Survey 25 inch map of the 1880s shows a pump on the edge of the green opposite the south-eastern corner of the churchyard.

There were several attempts in the 19th century to enclose a part of the green. They failed. The third attempt, in 1879, was described as "an attempt at depriving the parish of a very valuable source of recreation to them, as also it was to that numerous section of the Norwich public that found its summer pleasure for the most part on the river."

In 1855 the parishioners put down posts and rails to protect the green. In 1919 the lord of the manor gave the green to the parish council and a war memorial was erected there.

# THE BUCK
## FORMERLY THE WHITE LION

On the north side of the road, next to the church, is the Buck (Plate 20). This is a brick and flint building that descends in stages of height towards the road. There are four sections. The section furthest from the road is probably 17th century and has lucarne windows. The section adjoining this (now pierced by a modern porch) may be 18th century. The two sections nearest the road are probably 19th century, but may have been partly rebuilt. They contain flint particularly on the churchyard side. These two latter sections may have originated as outbuildings. A photograph of about 1880 shows that at that time there was no chimney and so these sections were unheated. The tenant of the Buck in the late 1870s was also a coal merchant. He advertised this with a sign on the gable end of the higher of these two sections: "COALS SOLD HERE". This suggests they were used in connection with his coal business. A coal business may also have been run from here in the 1840s and 1850s. The tenant at that time was referred to in 1850 as a "coal dealer".

Before about 1775 the Buck was known as the White Lion. It is clear from 18th century manor court rolls, that, below the north end of the building, there was a cellar. There was also a gate or gateway across a passage separating the Buck and its yard from the limekiln that lay to the north. From the churchyard wall to the eastern side of the yard of the Buck was 23 yards (21 metres). The owners of the limekiln had the right to transport materials through the yard to the road. They could leave and lay them on the 25 yards (23 metres) of staithe near the river over which the Buck had rights. The yard of the Buck comprised a walled enclosure east of the two lower sections of the building and a passageway that ran between the Buck and this enclosure. The wall around the enclosure was demolished in the 1920s, when a garage and stable were built there. The yard is now used as a car park.

In the 19th century the eastern half of the present car park was part of the neighbouring property – No. 63 Yarmouth Road. It was occupied by two buildings (Plate 20). Immediately west of and adjoining No. 63 was a building that was there by 1800, was a post office in 1901 and several years later was a cycle shop. West of that was a building set back from the road. It was there by 1800 and in 1841 was occupied by a shoe maker. From at least 1850 to the 1870s, it was a post office. In about 1905 this small building was demolished and a bigger, taller "Tudor-style" building with half-timbering was erected on the roadside (back cover). Both buildings were demolished in about 1960.

The track that ran along the eastern side of the Buck seems to have continued northwards as far as the Chapel Lane / South Avenue pit. In fact, before the pit blocked it, it may have continued northwards to Yarmouth Way.

# NUMBER 63 YARMOUTH ROAD
## FORMERLY THE HOMESTEAD

Before 1786, the property consisted of three-quarters of an acre of land and included a barn and other buildings on the site of what is now No. 67 Yarmouth Road. In 1786 what is now No. 67 Yarmouth Road was sold off.

In 1800 the property was described as "a Dwelling-House, Stable, and Cart, Chaise or Coach House, Two Cottages and about a quarter of an Acre of Land." The cottages were the two buildings that stood immediately west of No. 63 (see "The Buck" above). The 1841 tithe map shows that by then cottages had been built on the northern boundary of the site. In 1883, "Church Cottages" were built north-west of the house, divorcing it from its garden.

In 1993 Edwin Rose carried out an archaeological survey of the building. The basic structure consists of a line of four rooms. The earlier rooms are the rooms on either side of the central axial stack. The rooms at the north and south ends are later additions. It seems that the building began, probably in the late 16th century, as a small brick and flint building, now represented by the room south of the central stack. A date-stone of 1586 may relate to this, although it is not in its original position. In the early 17th century, a grand three-storey, timber-framed parlour block was added, to the north of the original building. It included a new or remodelled stack. It had a single storey extension to the north and possibly a cellar. The rooms at the north and south ends of the present building were added, probably in the 19th century, the south wall being rebuilt in 1880 by its then owner John Henry Piggott. The date-stone reads "JHP 1880".

It appears from the 1841 tithe map that at that time the house was divided into three dwellings. There may have been a shop or workshop in the middle section, because the occupier was described as "a grocer and a silversmith". In the 1871 census the building is referred to as "Dial House". By 1891 it was known as "The Homestead".

# NUMBER 67 YARMOUTH ROAD
## IDLE HOUR

In 1800 the building that stood on this site was described as "cottages". By the 1880s it is clear that it was divided into three, the largest unit being towards the north. The building extended southwards as far as the street and faced out to Chapel Lane. At the time of the 1861 census, part of the building was occupied by a "General Shopkeeper", who in 1871 was referred to as a baker and grocer. By 1881 it was a post office. By 1891, the post office had moved and the building was referred to as "Old Post Office Yard".

In the late 1890s, the cottages were pulled down, the western boundary was moved towards No. 63 and Idle Hour was built. Unlike the cottages, it was set back from the street. It was also wider than the cottages had been. In about 1920 the gable end at the front of the building was extended slightly and a northern extension was added.

An 1893 photograph of the southern end of the cottages shows that they were of flint with stone quoins. When the new house was built, the cottages were not demolished completely. Part of the eastern wall of the cottages and, probably, the cellars, were incorporated. This part of the eastern wall is irregular in construction and includes flint and brick. A manor court entry of 1786 suggests that some or all of the cottages had been part of a barn. Much of the fabric of the barn seems to have been retained when the conversion into cottages occurred in the 1790s. Some of it can be seen in the east wall of Idle Hour today.

# CHAPEL LANE

Chapel Lane may have originated as an access way to a chalk pit. A manor court entry of 1786 refers to it as "the way leading to the lime kiln in the use of William Brinded." Premises called the Lime Kilns are referred to in the vicinity in 1697. At the northern end of the lane, there appears to have been a quarry, with a later large pit dug into it on the eastern side. Before the Second World War, the pit used to come through as far as South Avenue. After the war, this part of the pit was filled in. It has now been built over.

Chapel Lane was named after a Congregationalist chapel that was built there in 1839 (Plate 21). The Reverend John Alexander, pastor of Princes Street Congregationalist Church, began the Thorpe Mission in 1829. The chapel that was built ten years later was also used as a day school. It had seats for 150. On Sundays there were afternoon and evening services. In 1851 there was an average congregation of 60 at each service. This compared with 105 at the church. The average Sunday school attendance at the chapel was 40 on a Sunday afternoon,

*Plate 21 : The parish hall (formerly a Congregationalist chapel), Chapel Lane, in 1987.*

compared with a combined morning and afternoon total of 93 at the church. In 1897 the chapel closed and was purchased by the church as a mission room and parish hall. It was demolished in the late 1980s. The site is now occupied by Nos. 8A to 8D Chapel Lane.

Opposite them are Nos. 12 and 14 Chapel Lane. At the time of the 1901 census, the building they occupy was a working-men's club. By the 1930s, it had been converted into two houses.

Probably the oldest buildings in the lane are the cottages north of Nos. 12 and 14 Chapel Lane. Their date-stone reads "KH 1820." "KH" was Roger Kerrison Harvey, John Harvey's third son. He is named as the owner of the cottages in the 1841 tithe records.

At that time, he also owned the row of flint and brick cottages that run off westwards at the end of Chapel Lane. By 1881 there were 11 of them, although the 1891 census only refers to 10. In that census, the row is referred to as "Rotten Row" – "rotten" suggesting soft yielding ground, possibly a reference to the quarry to the north, east and west.

The name Chapel Lane first appears in the 1851 census. Censuses from 1851 to 1881 also refer to all or part of the lane as "Green Hills".

# NUMBERS 69, 71, 73, 75 AND 77 YARMOUTH ROAD

Nos. 69 and 71/73 (Plate 22) are flint and brick cottages with single-storey extensions at the front. They were there in 1800. In 1841 No. 69 was a shoemakers and No.71/73 a bakery. The latter is now The River Bank Hair & Beauty. It was previously Krazy Daizies, a florist, and before then, Chris Denham, newsagent and general stores.

No. 75 is an end-on house that dates from at least 1800. 1841 tithe records show it was divided into three cottages. In 1891 the first one was the post office and the other two were called "Post Office Yard".

No. 77 is an 18th century house extended to the street in 1902, when Walter Parker built on a shop and lounge with a roof garden and bedroom above. This was the post office and general stores that Walter's sisters, brother and then nephew ran until the late 1950s. It is now The Café by the River and Harleys.

*Plate 22 : Nos. 69, 71/73, 75 and 77 Yarmouth Road and Dunollie (now Richmond Court), in about 1905.*

In 1697 all or part of Nos. 69-77 were part of a piece of land called the Lime Kilns.

Until South Avenue was constructed in the early 19<sup>th</sup> century, there was a row of cottages east of No. 77. A 1697 deed names four occupiers and says that the cottages were between land called the Lime Kilns on the west and a way called Englands Lane on the east.

# SOUTH AVENUE
## (INCLUDING HIGH HOUSE AND THE SITE OF THOMPSON'S FOLLY)

South Avenue probably originated between 1825 and 1840 as a private road that led to an early 19th century house now called "High House" (No. 91 Thunder Lane) and the farm that adjoined it to the north. However, there had been an earlier cartway or track called Englands Lane (see "Nos. 69, 71, 73, 75 and 77 Yarmouth Road" above).

The house and farm were built by Thomas Batley, a timber merchant. He acquired the site in 1801 and appears to have lived there until he died in 1840. Until about 1880 the house was called "the Grove". Batley retained an earlier farmhouse that stood nearby. In 1800 the earlier farm was described as a "Cottage, Barn, and other Buildings, and 45 Acres of Land". In the early 1790s it was owned and occupied by William Foster, an attorney at law, and in the late 1790s by Jehoshaphat Postle, a beer brewer.

In the 1860s the Grove was acquired by William Birkbeck. In 1871 Birkbeck employed Thomas Jeckyll to design a large extension and make other alterations to the house, including a wooden porch and possibly interiors. The earlier farmhouse may have been demolished at this time. In about 1880 the Grove was renamed "High House". At the end of the 19th century "lodges" were built - "North Lodge" (No. 93 Thunder Lane) in about 1880 on the line of Yarmouth Way, nearly opposite Hilly Plantation, and "South Lodge" in about 1910, near the bottom of South Avenue (No. 3).

Between South Avenue and Stanmore Road, there is evidence of a pit. In 1841 this was referred to as "the Dell". It is marked on the 1801 enclosure map and so is likely to date from at least the 18th century. The map shows it was accessed by a track that ran through what are now Nos. 81 and 83 Yarmouth Road.

On a hill in Weston Wood, near the end of Western Avenue, there used to be a round tower (Plate 23). In 1800 it was referred to as "Thompson's Folly" which suggests it was built in the 1750s or 1760s by John Thompson, or his son Nockold. Nockold was mayor of Norwich in 1759. They owned a large estate including the wood. Bardwell's 1760 painting appears to show it as a square [sic] tower with a roof. In 1783, Sylas Neville linked the tower with the rector, Richard Humfrey. Neville wrote in his diary:

> The parsonage commands the river & meadows with the road to Yarmouth, but from the grove behind, which is on a bank, there are a variety of delightful views.... there are none better than those from Mr Humphrey's Belvidere.... The river barges under sail, rich meadows and woods, country seats with mills etc. in picturesque situations.

Faden's map of Norfolk, surveyed in the early 1790s, refers to the tower as "Thorpe Gazebo" and shows an avenue of trees leading up to, and continuing around, it. Grigor, in 1841, refers to it as "a lonely watch-tower … almost clad with ivy". Part of the tower was still standing in the 1950s and is depicted in a small drawing in the Eastern Evening News of 13th August 1955. The tower was of flint and was said to have "three rooms, one on top of another". It is no longer visible.

*Plate 23 : The tower in Weston Wood ("Thompson's Folly")*
*photographed by Mr Nigel C C Bill in 1953.*

# RICHMOND COURT
## THE SITE OF DUNOLLIE

These flats were built in the 1930s on the site of a large 18th century house that had been known from at least 1891 as "Dunollie" (Plate 22). In 1800 it was owned by Barnabas Leman and occupied by Thomas Watson. The construction of South Avenue in the early 19th century gave Dunollie a bigger garden. It increased its grounds from 0.88 acres to 1.07 acres.

18th century copyhold deeds refer to a cartway on the western edge of the property and "an ancient footway now disused" on the northern boundary. The cartway gave access to the cottages that were east of No. 77 (see " Nos. 69, 71, 73, 75 and 77 Yarmouth Road" above).

# THE RUSHCUTTERS
## FORMERLY THE BOAT AND BOTTLE, PREVIOUSLY THORPE GARDENS, ORIGINALLY THE TUNS

*Plate 24 : Roadside view of the Tuns (now the Rushcutters) in 1874.*

On the other side of the road is the Rushcutters (Plates 24 and 25).

According to Stephen Heywood's 1998 survey, the building dates from about 1600. Its first-recorded owner, Thomas Gibson esquire of Thorpe, may have built it. His will was proved in 1616 (see also "The old church and the movement of the settlement" above).

Heywood identified a six-bay timber frame, with an original brick and flint east gable end, including an original stack. The two easternmost bays were the parlour and parlour chambers. The hall was probably in the two bays further west. The two westernmost bays may have contained the service rooms. The large western stack was probably added during the 17th century. In the middle of the 19th century the west crosswing was added.

Before 1800 this and the neighbouring property (now No. 48 Yarmouth Road) were a unit. A deed of 1745 describes them as a "Capital Messuage … and a Great Barn and Malting Office and House with a Cistern of Lead to the said Malting Office and House … and One Garden and Two Orchards and the back Grounds.. all inclosed with a Stone wall on the west, a Fleet of Water on the east and abutting on the Kings Highway on the north." Attached to the property were 100 acres of "bruery ground" (i.e. heath) called Gargett's Hills (see "The original church etc." below) and four acres of meadow. The tenant was John Miller, a maltster.

In 1800 what is now No. 48 Yarmouth Road was sold off. It was described as a "Malthouse" with "a Storehouse and Lean-to adjoining to the west." It was converted into a house. By 1900 it was known as Eastwick and it is now called Monk's Barn. In the 1930s the southern half of the building was demolished, including a wing that abutted the Rushcutters.

In 1800 the Rushcutters was described in a deed as a "Capital Messuage now used as a Public house and called … the Tuns … with Barns, Stables, Houses …Gardens, Bowling-Green." The tenant was Robert Cattermoul. Adjoining the buildings were two cottages. A Norwich directory of 1783 refers to a freemasons' lodge that met at the Tuns in Thorpe and was founded in 1766. It therefore appears to have been a public house since at least that date.

By 1825 the tenant was Thomas William Hinsby. James Stark's *"Hinsby's Gardens, Thorpe"* was published in 1829. This shows a very truncated view of the building, but it does illustrate that by this time the western half of the site had been laid out as a lawn with covered arbours or boxes on the north and east sides, that looked like cloisters.

*Plate 25 : Riverside view of Thorpe Gardens (now the Rushcutters) in about 1905, with, on the right, the "Het Varke" sign.*

In 1843 the present western crosswing was added. In September of that year there is a newspaper reference to Mr Cattermole's "splendid new room", which was the large clubroom on the first floor of the new wing. The eastern "cloister" of the lawn was incorporated within the ground floor of the new building. The ground floor was also used as skittle alley. The new wing had a sign on the roof - "CATTERMOLE", the name of the new proprietor, Robert Cattermole, probably the son of the tenant who had been there forty years before.

Following John Harvey's death in 1842, Cattermole was a leading light in the Thorpe Regatta and races took place from the Tuns. When this was advertised in the Norwich Mercury of 9th July 1842, the advertisement included an engraving of a rowing boat, a yacht in front and a silver cup in the sky. Superimposed on the picture was a boar under which were the words "Het Varke". This is the sign that from about the 1850s until 1969 hung over the back door of the public house facing the river (Plate 25). It was a blue pig with golden tusks, with the words "Het Varke" inscribed beneath. "Het Varke" is Dutch for "this pig". It was suggested by Hooper (Eastern Daily Press 19th November 1895) that it was a "relic probably of some ill-fated Batavian coaster, lost or broken on East Anglian shores." There is better explanation.

Thomas Vere was lord of the manor of Thorpe from 1751 until 1766. His family crest matches the sign, because it is described as "a boar passant azure attired or". There is no evidence that the Veres ever owned the building or lived there. The earliest photograph of the Tuns, taken in about 1845, does not show the sign. It appears first on a slightly later photograph, probably taken in the 1850s. Vere's school was closed in 1841 (see "Ferryman's Court" above). Cattermole may have acquired the sign from there.

By 1883 the name of the inn had changed to Thorpe Gardens. A plan of 1888 shows the site was split into two areas. In the western half were the gardens with a lawn in middle and terraces and seats (some sheltered) around it. In the eastern half was the public house facing the river with seats in front of it. By the date of the plan, the skittle alley had become a boathouse. Behind the public house was a yard, with stables and a kitchen garden and access from the road.

By the 1920s (i.e. between 1912 and 1926) the "cloister" on the northern side of lawn had been demolished. During the 1930s the short eastern extension to the main block, that may have once been a cottage, also went. In 1956, as part of road widening, the northern boundary of the lawn area was moved further south. In 1969 the name of the public house was changed to the Boat and Bottle and, in 1985, it changed again to the Rushcutters.

# NUMBER 87 YARMOUTH ROAD

On the opposite side of the road to the Rushcutters is No. 87 Yarmouth Road. This large late 18th century house has a pilastered classical south door. In 1800 it was owned by the beer brewer Jehoshaphat Postle and occupied by William White. Postle and his father before him (of the same name) owned the Rushcutters (then the Tuns) from 1754 until 1800. In 1841 Postle's widow, Sarah, was living at No. 87 with two daughters and five servants. Of the houses along Yarmouth Road in 1841, this number of servants was only exceeded by John Harvey at Thorpe Lodge who had ten and Charles Weston at Thorpe House who had six.

In the 20th century the house was known as "the Dell". In 1956 the stables and part of the south wing were reduced in size, when the road was widened.

# GIRLING'S LANE
## (INCLUDING THE SITE OF THE RAILWAY ACCIDENT)

On the other side of the road is Girling's Lane. Near the end of the lane is a railway crossing. The Yarmouth and Norwich Railway was opened on 30th April 1844, work having begun on the track a year earlier. To accommodate the railway, bridges were built across the river south of Thorpe Hall and south of the Rushcutters. To avoid having two opening bridges within a mile, a channel was excavated from Trowse Hythe to Whitlingham Reach, known as the New Cut. From that time, this was the main route used by river traffic.

Just before the railway crossing on Girling's Lane, there is a commemorative stone, recording the tragic railway accident that occurred here on 10th September 1874. An express train from Norwich collided with a mail train from Brundall. The drivers and the firemen of both locomotives were killed. Eighteen passengers were killed on the spot, and about fifty were severely wounded, five of whom died during the next few days. The dead and the dying were taken to the Tuns (now the Rushcutters), and the injured to the Norfolk and Norwich Hospital.

Girling's Lane is named after the boat hirers and builders who, in the 1920s and 1930s, had a boatyard on the far side of the railway line.

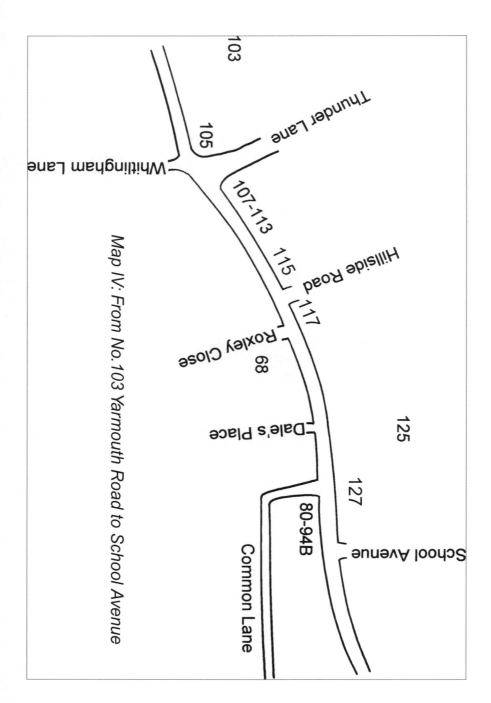

Map IV: From No.103 Yarmouth Road to School Avenue

103

105

Thunder Lane

Whitlingham Lane

107-113

115

Hillside Road

117

Roxley Close

68

Dale's Place

125

127

School Avenue

80-94B

Common Lane

# IV: From No. 103 Yarmouth Road to School Avenue

## NUMBER 103 YARMOUTH ROAD
### THE OLD RECTORY

On the other side of the road is No. 103 Yarmouth Road. Although there have been alterations, this is essentially the rectory that was built in 1754. It is of brick and has five bays and three storeys.

A memorandum in the parish register by Richard Humfrey, rector of Thorpe from 1753 until 1813, reads:

> 1754 - The Parsonage House, having been entirely taken down and rebuilt, was finished this Year and the Wash-house rebuilt, the Barn new thatched with reed, the South End of the Stable built, the Hay Chamber Floor, the Partitions, Rack, Manger, etc. were all put up new and the stable paved, large new doors made to the Hay-house and the whole put in good repair. The Garden on the South side of the House was also made this year... wall next to the Road built and the Gates... put up all new.

A glebe terrier of 1763 refers to the house as having "two parlours, hall, study, kitchen with chamber and garrets over". It also refers to "two barns, a stable and other outhouses".

According to the rector's accounts:

> Sept 12 1754 Paid for a Stone to put up at East end of House with the Date when it was built 3s.
> Nov 16 1754 Paid for a Roof-raising Treat to the Workmen that built the new Parsonage £1 9s 9d.

A 1692 terrier includes a description of the previous rectory. It contained "one Kitchen, one Buttery or Pantry with an entry on the south side, one Hall, one Parlour with Chambers of a second storey over each and a third storey except over the Hall." This suggests a timber-framed house with a hall open to the roof in the middle, service rooms (with rooms over them) and an entry at one end and a parlour (with rooms over it) at the other end.

From descriptions of 1692 and 1699, it appears there was a large stone barn 90 feet (27.5 metres) in length and 20 feet (6 metres) in breadth. There was a timber-framed hay-house at the north end and a "lading" or shed at the south end. On the west side was a timber-framed dairy. There was also a smaller barn of 27 feet (8 metres) by 21 feet (6.5 metres) with a stable and pigsties and a cattle-shed with a hay chamber over them at the south end and a cart house at the end of them.

As mentioned under "No. 53 Yarmouth Road" above, in 1863 the rectory changed hands as part an exchange of land between William Birkbeck and the church. In 1872 Birkbeck sold it to Charlotte Herring, widow of Armine Herring, rector of Thorpe from 1857 until 1867.

East of the former rectory is a former coach-house that, from map evidence, was built between 1841 and the 1880s.

# NUMBER 105 YARMOUTH ROAD
## FORMERLY THE WHITE HOUSE

Although it has been altered, the present house is basically a late 18th century house, with a shaped gable and blocked windows at the rear, that appear to be remnants of a 17th century house. It seems from the 1800 enclosure map that the 18th century house was built as a southern extension of the 17th century house. By the 1880s there had been numerous changes to the house, which may have obliterated much of the 17th century building. A modern brick extension has been attached to the east front of the building.

A clue to the early development of the house comes with its link to the Johnson charity. William Johnson, an apothecary from Arminghall, owned the property in about 1700. He wanted to extend his garden eastwards and so take in some of Thunder Lane. This he did and it explains the kink that used to be in Thunder Lane at the junction with Yarmouth Road. (The kink was removed when, in 1959, the road was widened and an old oak tree removed). It was agreed that in compensation for taking in some of the roadway, Johnson should pay the churchwardens and overseers of the parish £1 a year. When he died in 1705, aged 74, the money became a rentcharge on his house. According to an 1839 Charity Commissioners report, the money was used at Christmas to buy "threepenny loaves" for the "poorest persons of the parish". In a survey of between 1700 and 1731 there is a reference to "Johnson" at "Halfway house". This may be an earlier name for the house.

A manor court roll of 1785 refers to the house as being "formerly Yallops". According to an inscription in the church, Robert Yallop "died at his house in this town 28th July 1656 aged 55". He was buried in the old church. He was the father of Sir Robert who acquired the manor of Bowthorpe in 1660, was knighted in 1664 and died in 1705 aged 68. Sir Robert was a Catholic. If Robert his son was also a Catholic, he would have not been alone in Thorpe in the 17th century. Edward

Paston and his grandson Clement were Catholics, as was Robert Blofeld, rector of Thorpe from 1642 until 1670.

In 1800 the house was described as a "farmhouse" that had "several barns, outhouses and other buildings and 216 acres of land". It was owned and occupied by Isaac Marsh. From the 1860s the house was known as Covey House. It was later named the White House.

By 1830 the buildings immediately north of the house (now No. 1 Thunder Lane and an access way to No. 103 Yarmouth Road) were being used as a tannery. During the 1860s what in 1841 had been Golding Allen's "Tan Office and premises" had become a yard with cottages on the north and east sides and the outbuildings of the then rectory on the west side. By 1891 there were 14 cottages in "Tan Yard", which was also known as Albert Place (Plate 26). Two of them had only two rooms, three had three rooms and the others had four rooms.

*Plate 26 : Albert Place (formerly Tan Yard) in 1953 (now No.1 Thunder Lane and an access to No. 103 Yarmouth Road).*

# WHITLINGHAM LANE

On the other side of the road is Whitlingham Lane. This is so-called because, until the 1840s, you could walk along the lane, crossing the meadow, continue south along a riverside path until the eastward bend in the river and then cross the river by ferry to Whitlingham. In 1845, the ferry was run by Ann King, keeper of the White House tavern in Trowse, close to the Whitlingham parish boundary.

White's Norfolk of 1845 describes Whitlingham thus:

> The church (St Andrew) was dilapidated about 1630, and now forms a picturesque ruin, near the verge of a lofty precipice, overlooking the river. The tavern called Whitlingham White House is in Trowse Newton parish, and has a ferry across the Yare. Pleasure parties often visit this spot to enjoy its romantic scenery and remarkable echo.

In 1869 Bayne wrote in his History of Norwich:

> The road from the Foundry bridge to Thorpe village is a favourite walk of the citizens [of Norwich]. .... On the south side of the river, which was once reached by the ferry boat, stands the village of Whitlingham, where the citizens formerly resorted by thousands in the summer months. The grounds in this locality present a pleasing variety of hill and dale, wood and water, and the view from the White House includes the windings of the 'bonny Yare,' the opposite village of Thorpe, [and, in Norwich,] the spire of the Cathedral and the frowning aspect of the old Norman Castle.

The White House tavern was an Italianate building that in the 1860s Sir Robert John Harvey demolished and rebuilt as a thatched cottage (also known as the White House).

The 12th century round tower of Whitlingham church collapsed in 1940.

According to Robinson and Rose, Thunder Lane is part of a Roman road between Brampton and Thorpe. There may have been a Romano-

British riverside settlement at Thorpe. Whitlingham Lane and the ferry-crossing appear to be a continuation of Thunder Lane. This suggests that Whitlingham Lane, and possibly the ferry crossing, are of a similar age to Thunder Lane.

In 1844 the railway line crossed Whitlingham Lane. Whitlingham Station was opened in 1874, as part of the development of the adjacent Whitlingham junction from which a new line branched off to North Walsham. This was extended, three years later, to Cromer. Whitlingham Station closed to passenger services in 1955 and general goods in 1964. It stood immediately east of the footbridge, erected over the line in 1886, and on the north side of the line.

# THUNDER LANE

On the other side of the road to Whitlingham Lane is Thunder Lane. It may have originated as a Roman road (see "Whitlingham Lane" above). Its continued importance during the medieval period and up to 1801 was as a drove way for taking cattle and sheep to and from Mousehold Heath. On the 1589 Mousehold map, it is called Drovegate. Until 1801, Thunder Lane crossed Yarmouth Way just south of Hilly Plantation and entered Mousehold Heath just south of Laundry Close. In the 1801 Thorpe enclosure award the existing road is called both Thunder Lane and Sheeps Path Lane. Thunder Lane probably continued as a track across the heath. When Mousehold was turned into fields in 1801, the track was straightened and made into a road.

Thunder Lane is probably named after the Thunder family who owned property in Thorpe in the late 15th and early 16th centuries. The will of John Thundir [sic] of Thorpe was proved in 1500.

Yarmouth Way may be the hollow way running through the front gardens of Nos. 17, 18 and 19 Hilly Plantation. However, the 1801 enclosure award says that the road now called Hilly Plantation was part of Yarmouth Way – see Appendix 2, "East-west roads", below. To the east are allotments that are accessible from Hillside Avenue. If you imagine Yarmouth Way running through the northern end of the allotments, it would pass the site of the first church of Thorpe St Andrew.

# THE ORIGINAL CHURCH AND SETTLEMENT

In May 1951 Mr D W Aldous was planting potatoes in a newly-cleared allotment just east of Hilly Plantation. He noticed some masonry and bone fragments but assumed they were from muck spreading. Then his dog found a human jaw. He had discovered a church that had been forgotten for at least 300 years. Rose and Davison subsequently identified this as the first church of Thorpe St Andrew.

A P Baggs, R R Clarke and A J Martin excavated the site at intervals from 1951 until 1953 (Plate 27). The earliest evidence was of late Saxon

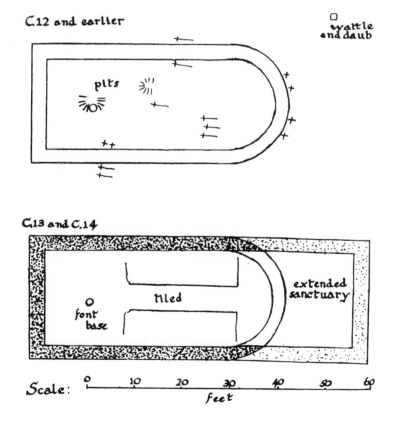

*Plate 27 : Plans of the original church, drawn following the 1951-53 excavations.*

domestic occupation, with refuse pits containing pottery, loom-weights and a decorated silver pinhead of Viking type. In the 11th century the site had been used as a burial ground. Some of the burials were then disturbed, probably in the early 12th century, by the construction of a single-celled, apsidal-ended church that was 55 feet (17 metres) by 25 feet (7.5 metres), including walls 3 feet (1 metre) thick, a font and possibly red floor tiles. Probably in the early 13th century, a rectangular chancel with poor foundations was added to the church, extending the total length of the building to 70 feet (21.5 metres). By the 14th century the nave floor was covered with tiles with yellow, red and green glaze, and the chancel screen (described in "The old church etc" above) had been built.

The late Saxon domestic occupation is important evidence of post-Roman occupation of Thorpe. As well as the pits, a wattle and daub building was found that was either late Saxon or early Norman. In

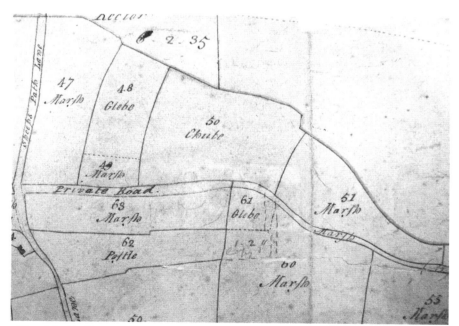

*Plate 28 : Fields near the original church from the 1800 enclosure map. Near the middle of the map is 61 Glebe. This is the original churchyard. To the north of it is Yarmouth Way.*

Thorpe, late Saxon pottery has also been discovered just north of No. 16 Harvey Lane (The Oaks), which is also not far south of Yarmouth Way. Late Saxon (as well as 13th/14th century) pottery has also been found near where the path from Whitlingham Lane first reaches the river, in other words, after the dyke. This suggests a place where goods were loaded and unloaded.

It is tempting to link the 11th century burial ground with Stigand. He is the first-recorded lord of the manor of Thorpe. He was bishop of East Anglia from 1042 and was probably granted Thorpe by Edward the Confessor at that time, although he may have received it earlier since he had been an influential royal adviser since at least 1020.

In 1101 Henry I granted the manor of Thorpe to Herbert de Losinga, bishop of Norwich. The bishops of Norwich had a manor house at Thorpe, at least from the first half of the 14th century. De Losinga was a great church-builder and was responsible for the construction of Norwich Cathedral Priory and the priory churches of St Nicholas, Great Yarmouth and St Margaret, Kings Lynn. It is highly likely that he built the original church at Thorpe. It may have been the last in a series of churches he constructed along the edge of Mousehold Heath. It would have followed on from Magdalen Chapel (now the Lazar House, Sprowston Road), St. Michael's Chapel and St Leonard's Priory.

The original church was immediately south of Yarmouth Way and east of what is now No. 19 Hilly Plantation. After passing the church, Yarmouth Way turned east-south-eastwards and ran down towards where the railway bridge now crosses Yarmouth Road. It then turned eastwards to the boundary with Postwick (Plate 43).

Thorpe's first church was a roadside church, about 170 yards (155 metres) south of Mousehold Heath (Plate 28). Its position suggests that the village of Thorpe grew up along Yarmouth Way – perhaps between near where Yarmouth Way crossed Thunder Lane at "North Lodge" (No. 93 Thunder Lane) and where it crossed what is now Pound Lane.

The 1589 Mousehold map shows that the land west of Thunder Lane and between Yarmouth Way and Mousehold Heath was demesne land, meaning that it belonged to the lord of the manor. This increases the possibility that the manor house site was nearby.

Between the original church and what is now Pound Lane, Yarmouth Way ran down east-south-eastwards along what are now the northern boundaries of the allotments and Hillside Avenue Primary and Nursery School. It then continued in the same direction between Highfield Close and St Andrew's Close, crossing Pound Lane immediately south of the Sainsbury's site. North of this part of Yarmouth Way was an area of Mousehold Heath of about 100 acres known as Gargytt Hills (the 1589 Mousehold map), Gargett Hills (the 1600 Mousehold map), Gargett's Hills (a 1745 title deed for the Rushcutters) or Gargate holes, hole or hill (the 1841 tithe map). If the correct form is Gargate, it may be an alternative name for Yarmouth Way, the prefix "gar" being linked with earlier forms of the name of the River Yare. It is also possible that it was a name that was associated with the settlement that grew up along this part of Yarmouth Way. (An area of woodland north of the Ring Road that in 1841 was called Gargate hill plantation has since at least the 1880s been called "Garglehill Plantation").

Thorpe is depicted on the 1600 Mousehold map (Plate 40). The part of Thorpe east of Thunder Lane seems to have a different character from the rest of the parish. It is only in this part of Thorpe that you find an open field, the low riverside common and, across the river, the parish of Whitlingham. This may, in part, be because of changes to the landscape west of Thunder Lane. Field boundaries on the 1800 enclosure map (Plate 42) suggest that, before these changes, between Thunder Lane and what is now Dale's Loke / Bishop's Close, there was an open field. Between Dale's Loke / Bishop's Close and Harvey Lane, there were irregular fields, probably taken in from woodland in the 13th or 14th century (see "Thorpe Hall - Description and history before 1535" above). By the time of the 1600 Mousehold map, the whole area had been converted largely to pasture, either enclosed or left open to Mousehold. This change probably happened in the 15<sup>th</sup> or 16<sup>th</sup> century, when pasture land became profitable through the growth in demand for wool.

There may once have been a link between the churches of Thorpe and Whitlingham. Both churches are dedicated to St Andrew, as are Trowse to the west of Whitlingham and Kirby Bedon to the south. Whitlingham church is situated on a hill and is mentioned in Domesday. It may have been Thorpe's "mother-church".

The church at Thorpe lacked aisles or a tower. This suggests a poor community who could not afford to add to their church. It may also suggest a small community that did not need a larger church for a growing population. The principal change to the church was the extension and squaring of the chancel in the early 13<sup>th</sup> century. This was the date ascribed to the masonry mass found at the time of the excavation. Since the chancel was the responsibility of the rector or patron (the bishop of Norwich), he rather than the parish, would have been responsible for extending it, probably to provide more liturgical space.

Although the bishop had a major house in the parish, there is no suggestion that, (apart from appointing priests), he had any major involvement in the church. For reasons mentioned under "Thorpe Hall - Description and history before 1535" above, it is likely that in the 13<sup>th</sup> or 14<sup>th</sup> century, the bishop's manor house was established at Thorpe Hall, about a mile from the church. By the early 14<sup>th</sup> century, the bishop's manor house had its own chapel.

At some point in the first half of the 16th century, it was decided to move the church down what is now Thunder Lane and westwards along what is now Yarmouth Road to its present site opposite River Green (see "The old church and the movement of the settlement" above). The 1950s excavation showed that the original church was systematically destroyed in the 16<sup>th</sup> century when all walls and foundations (except those of the Norman apse) were removed.

# THE THUNDER LANE / YARMOUTH ROAD JUNCTION

There have been several changes to the junction between Thunder Lane and Yarmouth Road. The first was the creation in the 16th century of the part of Yarmouth Road between Thunder Lane and just past the railway bridge (see "The old church and the movement of the settlement" above). The second was the extension in about 1700 of the garden of No. 105 (see "No. 105 Yarmouth Road" above).

Before the 16th century, the road that Yarmouth Road met just east of Whitlingham Lane was Common Lane. Now Common Lane does not begin until No. 127 Yarmouth Road. Until a date between 1825 and 1836 it continued westwards to the Thunder Lane junction (see Plates 41 and 43).

When the part of Yarmouth Road between Thunder Lane and just past the railway bridge was created, it did not meet the other part of Yarmouth Road at the Thunder Lane junction. Instead, the part between No. 68 Yarmouth Road and the junction ran further to the north than it does today. It went north of what are now Nos. 107, 109, 111, and 113 Yarmouth Road and came out on to Thunder Lane opposite what was then the farmyard behind No. 105 Yarmouth Road, and is now the garage of No. 1 Thunder Lane. (It may then have joined a footpath that until the 18th century appears to have run behind the properties on the north side of Yarmouth Road as far west at least as the church and possibly Dale's Loke - see "Richmond Court" above). In 1769 the road was moved south to create the present junction. It may be that, at the same time, a milestone was placed next to the garden wall of No. 105 Yarmouth Road, opposite Whitlingham Lane. It was two miles from Norwich and 20 miles from Yarmouth. It was still there in the 1930s.

The junction was widened in 1959 (see "No. 105 Yarmouth Road" above).

# NUMBERS 107-117 (ODD NUMBERS) AND NUMBER 68 YARMOUTH ROAD

Nos. 107 and 109 are a pair of flint cottages with steep roofs that may date from about 1700. Nos. 111 and 113 appear to date from the 19th century, although the flint in No. 111 may suggest that it incorporates an earlier building.

In 1841 the cottages were in the same ownership as No. 105 Yarmouth Road, on the opposite corner of Thunder Lane.

No. 115 is one of a group of early 20th century houses. It includes Nos. 1 to 5 and 2 to 8 Hillside Road. They are of red brick with some half-timbering and Dutch gables of various designs. Until it was demolished, the group also included No. 117 Yarmouth Road. That house has been replaced by a block of flats that reflects some of the features of the group.

On the other side of Yarmouth Road, immediately east of Roxley Close, is No. 68 Yarmouth Road. This was formerly Roxley House. It dates from the 1880s and was first associated with William Thomas Fisher Jarrold, a partner in Jarrold & Sons, publishers, booksellers, printers and stationers.

*Plate 29 : On the left, the sign of the Red Lion with a farm building, and, on the right, Dales Place, with Common Lane and No.80 onwards Yarmouth Road beyond, in about 1915.*

# NUMBER 127 YARMOUTH ROAD
## RAJ OF INDIA RESTAURANT FORMERLY THE RED LION

No. 127 was built as the Red Lion between 1830 and 1841. In 1841 it was in the same ownership as No. 105 Yarmouth Road. Opposite it lies Common Lane and to the east School Avenue. In 2002 the Red Lion was converted into a restaurant. It is now an Indian restaurant called the Raj of India.

Where the car park is now found (east of the No. 127), there used to be farm buildings that seem to have been contemporary with the public house (Plate 29). Oral evidence suggests that, before the First World War and for a while afterwards, the Red Lion was a beer house and a common lodging house, where drovers stayed overnight. The drovers would have been bringing cattle in from the Acle marshes to Norwich market.

West of No. 127 is No. 125 Yarmouth Road (Forge Cottage). It was built between 1825 and 1841. Its name suggests it was the site of a smithy, presumably linked with the farm.

Field boundaries on the 1800 enclosure map (Plate 43) suggest that there may have been a north/south track immediately west of No. 127. From here it may have run northwards close to what are now a north/south stretch of Meadow Lane and the southern entrance to the allotments. It may have continued northwards along the western boundary of the allotments and the western edge of the original churchyard (see "The original church and settlement" above) to Yarmouth Way. North of Yarmouth Way, it may have followed "the olde Churche pathe" (shown on the 1589 Mousehold map) to Mousehold Heath. South of No. 127, the track may have joined the short north/south stretch of Common Lane, although this is slightly to the east of the suggested route of the track.

# FROM THE "DALES PLACE" SIGN TO COMMON LANE
## THE SITE OF THE THIRD POORHOUSE

Opposite Nos. 125 and 127 Yarmouth Road and immediately west of Common Lane are some modern houses. They stand on the site of what was between 1782 and 1834 the village poorhouse or "town house". This was "for the maintenance and employment of such poor persons belonging to the parish as" were "unable to maintain themselves". An existing house was "fitted up" as a workhouse. There were two rooms on the ground floor and a chamber and garrets above. Along the east side of the building was a lean-to with a pantry and one other room on the ground floor and a large chamber above them. At the north end of the building, there was a wash-house. The premises also included a stable or outhouse, a garden and a yard.

Supple (pages 99-100) describes the life of the poor living in the town house. They were supervised by a matron. The doors were closed at 9pm and nobody was admitted after that time. If anyone got drunk or behaved in a disorderly manner, they were taken into custody by the parish constable and had to appear before a magistrate. In January 1796 the high cost of corn and other provisions led to changes in the diet of those living in the town house. Rice replaced wheat-flour and, as far as possible, potatoes replaced bread. On Mondays dinner was meat broth thickened with rice. On Wednesdays and Fridays dinner consisted of potatoes and red herrings. Where bread was given, it was made with half wheat meal and half barley flour mixed together.

In 1834 the poor living in the town house were moved to the new Union workhouse at Lingwood. The town house site was purchased by Robert Dale, a timber merchant, who built cottages there. It appears from the 1825 river map that No. 7 Dales Place was the site of the old town house building. A date stone in a wall reads "Dales Place 1841". By 1861 there were 13 cottages in "Dales Place" (Plate 29). In 1891 two of them had just one room, five had two rooms, one had three rooms, four had four rooms and one had at least five rooms.

At the end of the north-south stretch of Common Lane is an old wall and tucked around the corner facing the river is No. 12 Common Lane. This is now called Roxley Cottage but was previously called Larkhall Place. In the 1840s it was owned by John Rayner, a market gardener. He was keen to guard his property rights against his neighbour, Robert Dale. This is why there was a precise inscription on what was referred to as the Larkhall Place pillar. Today the inscription "JR 1846" can be seen on a stone in a brick pillar, probably a boundary marker.

# COMMON LANE
## (INCLUDING THE SITE OF THE SECOND POORHOUSE)

Common Lane may mark the original northern boundary of the common. It was also the boundary between the common pasture and the common field. The lane may have arisen in stages progressing eastwards as more of the common was enclosed. Running south from Common Lane, there was a track south of the Willows (even numbers 110-128 Yarmouth Road). This may mark an earlier edge of the common, or it may simply be an access way to the common. The earliest maps (the 1700 / 1731 sketch maps) show the western boundary of the common in the same place as it was on enclosure in 1863, in other words, the line of Bungalow Lane. Therefore Bungalow Lane may mark what had always been the boundary between common pasture (i.e. the "common") to the east and common meadow to the west. (For more on how the route of Common Lane has changed, see "The Thunder Lane / Yarmouth Road junction" above).

The track referred to above that ran south from Common Lane (south of the Willows) was also important in the development of Thorpe's poorhouse or "town house". In 1769 the town house moved from River Green to a site that had the track to the west and Common Lane to the north. It was divided into four tenements. As mentioned above under "From the 'Dales Place' sign to Common Lane", the town house moved again in 1782.

# NUMBERS 80-94B (EVEN NUMBERS) YARMOUTH ROAD
## THE SITE OF A TANNERY

These houses, opposite what is now School Avenue, mark the former site of a tannery. In 1800 it was described as a "House with Tan office, outbuildings, Cottages, Yards and Gardens" owned by Jane Smith, occupied by William Smith and of 1.329 acres. The 1800 enclosure map shows a large building on the site that may have been a drying shed.

An 1830 directory lists William Smith and Thomas Batley, both of Thorpe, as tanners. Smith seems to have been operating from this site and Batley from the site north of No. 105 Yarmouth Road. Norwich Castle Museum & Art Gallery has a watercolour by John Thirtle called *"A Tanyard, Thorpe near Norwich"*. It was first exhibited in 1808. It appears to be of Smith's tanyard since the road slopes down in front of the tanyard, which is on the right of the road. Smith's tannery had gone by 1841 and Batley's probably by 1845.

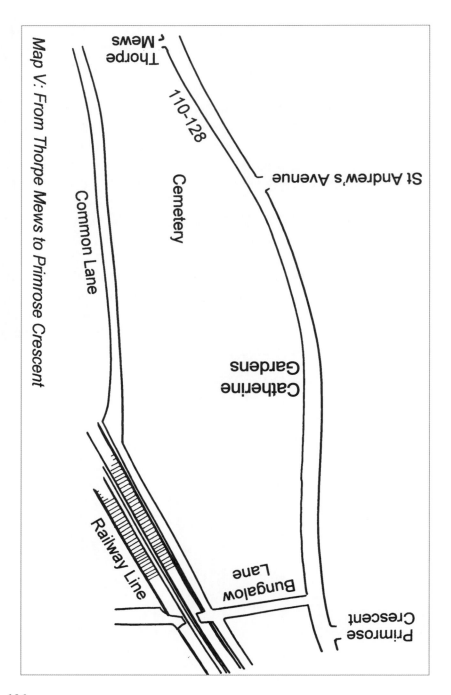

Map V: From Thorpe Mews to Primrose Crescent

# V: From Thorpe Mews to Primrose Crescent

## NUMBERS 110-128 (EVEN NUMBERS) YARMOUTH ROAD (THE WILLOWS) AND THE CEMETERY

In 1800 there were no buildings on either side of the road between what are now Nos. 80-94B (even numbers) Yarmouth Road and the railway bridge. The position was the same in 1841 and only slightly different by the 1880s. By then, on the south side of the road were a cemetery and a terrace called the Willows.

The churchyard ceased to be used for burials in 1858, when an acre of land was purchased as a cemetery and, in the following year, a small mortuary chapel was built (Plate 30). The cost was £250. At the same time, the asylum (see "St Andrew's Park" below) purchased the same amount of land for use as a cemetery immediately west of the church's plot. The chapel was demolished in 1973. The cemetery was extended eastwards in 1977.

*Plate 30 : The cemetery and mortuary chapel in about 1905.*

# BUNGALOW LANE AND THE COMMON

The common was known as the Low or Wet Common (Plate 43), as distinct from the high and dry common of Mousehold Heath. As mentioned above under "Common Lane", Bungalow Lane formed the western boundary of the common from at least the early 18th century until the common was enclosed in 1863. The common extended eastwards to Boundary Lane and a ditch that formed Thorpe's eastern boundary. The southern boundary of the common was the river. The northern boundary was just behind the properties fronting Yarmouth Road.

Under an 1803 agreement, there were 89 "goings" or rights to graze a beast on the common. Rights were attached to certain properties. For example, in 1741, John Bunting, the tenant of the King's Head, had the right to pasture two beasts on the common. However, by 1810, common rights were being sold separately from properties.

Horses, cows and one or two bulls were allowed to graze on the common from 13th May until the following 1st February. On 13th May and 1st February the parish bells rang between nine and twelve in the morning to signify the beginning or ending of the grazing season. There were two ways into or out of the common. One was along Common Lane, the other was next to what is now the northern end of Griffin Lane. It seems likely from the 1800 enclosure map that this northern entrance had once been a wide way immediately west of Griffin Lane.

The 1841 tithe map also shows that by this time the common was divided into four pieces - a major section of just over 60 acres, a riverside stretch of just over 6 acres and smaller pieces of 1.2 and 0.5 acres. The 89 common rights were divided among 11 common right owners. The two major owners were Sarah Batley with 24 rights and John Harvey with 21.

In 1843/4 the new Norwich to Yarmouth railway line was built across the common.

In 1863 the common was enclosed and divided amongst those who had rights over it. What is now Griffin Lane was extended eastwards to give access to the new enclosures. Another new road (Bungalow Lane) was built along what had been the western edge of the common.

In 1865 work began on the new railway line between Norwich and North Walsham. Work was halted in 1866 and was not completed until 1874. The line was built to the west of the old common and led to the diversion of Common Lane away from the common and along the north-western side of the railway track.

At the time of the 1871 census, there were families living in 5 tents on the former common. There was a travelling musician, a brazier, a hawker, a horse dealer and a cane chair mender.

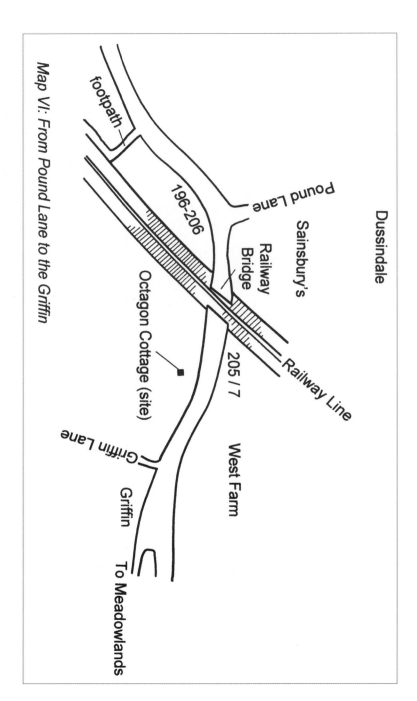

Map VI: From Pound Lane to the Griffin

# VI: From Pound Lane to the Griffin

## POUND LANE

Pound Lane was built in 1801 as a private road between the newly-created fields on what until then had been Mousehold Heath. Before 1801 the heath began just south of where the Ring Road now joins Pound Lane. Immediately south of the Sainsbury's site is where Yarmouth Way would have crossed what is now Pound Lane and then continued east-south-eastwards to the other side of what is now the railway bridge.

When it was first built, Pound Lane did not continue southwards as now, but followed the edge of Mousehold Heath south-eastwards until it met Yarmouth Road (Plate 43). By the 1830s this route had been abandoned and the present southern route established. Until the late 1860s, Pound Lane continued further southwards than now, meeting Yarmouth Road behind what is now Rowena Terrace (even numbers 196-206 Yarmouth Road).

On the eastern side of the junction with Yarmouth Road was the village pound, a small rectangular enclosure where stray animals were confined and only released on payment of a fine. It first appears on the 1841 tithe map and must have replaced the pound that in 1800 was near where the track west of No. 13 Yarmouth Road joins the road (see "Between Thorpe Lodge and No. 25 Yarmouth Road" above). In 1868 the pound at the end of Pound Lane was offered to the East Norfolk Railway Company for £40. This was in connection with the building of the new railway line to North Walsham and the consequent movement further northwards of the part of Yarmouth Road that had previously run in a straight line east-north-eastwards from Bungalow Lane to just east of the railway bridge.

The Sainsbury's supermarket was opened in 1989 and a new community centre, the Dussindale Centre, in 1990. Before 1801 the site was part of Mousehold Heath. By 1810 there was a marl pit and a limekiln there. At a manor court in 1836, a complaint was made that, since acquiring the site in 1820, John Harvey had dug and sold "divers quantities of Marle" from the land and had "burnt divers quantities of chalk into lime and sold the same without permission." In 1938-9 the site of a Romano-British pottery kiln was discovered. It was dated to the early second century.

Nearly a mile along Pound Lane is the Oasis Sports and Leisure Club. This was formerly "The Woodlands". The building dates from about 1860 and is first associated with Charles Jecks, a timber merchant. In 1864 it was described as "pleasantly situated in well wooded grounds in which is a small lake" (see also "Dussindale" below).

*Plate 31 : Octagon Cottage in the 1960s.*

# NUMBERS 205 AND 207 YARMOUTH ROAD, WEST FARM (NUMBERS 213 AND 215 YARMOUTH ROAD), THE GRIFFIN AND THE SITE OF OCTAGON COTTAGE

On the east side of the railway bridge, on the north side of the road, are Nos. 205 and 207 Yarmouth Road. They are a pair of brick and tile cottages with a half-flint gable end. They date from the early 19th century. Until the 1990s, on the opposite side of the road to them there was a curious octagonal building called Octagon Cottage or the Round House (Plate 31). It was not a toll-house. In 1803 it was described as "a new cottage built on land belonging to Sir Roger Kerrison". It was a double cottage of flint and red brick with pointed "Gothic-style" windows and doors. At about the same time, Kerrison built another two-storied octagonal cottage – also called the Round House – on Newmarket Road, Cringleford. This is of brick and has survived.

Octagon Cottage, Yarmouth Road, was built at an important road junction and next to where the common met Mousehold Heath. Enclosure, road diversions and road closures have altered very much how the area appeared at the beginning of the 19th century (see Plates 41 and 43).

Before Mousehold Heath was enclosed in 1801, the heath came down to the road between what is now the boundary between Nos. 207 and 209 Yarmouth Road and the eastern edge of the farm buildings (i.e. West Farm formerly Lime Kiln Farm now Nos. 213 and 215 Yarmouth Road). Yarmouth Way came down from the west-north-west and reached what is now Yarmouth Road also near the boundary between Nos. 207 and 209 Yarmouth Road. Yarmouth Road came up from the west-south-west emerging just south of the railway bridge and reaching the present Yarmouth Road just west of what was Octagon Cottage, close to where Yarmouth Way came down from the west-north-west. Cutting between the heath to the north and the way to the common to the south, Yarmouth Road followed its present course until immediately past West Farm. Here, it went past the present site of the Griffin and continued east-south-eastwards, passing just 30 yards (27 metres) from what became the front of the main buildings of St Andrew's Hospital (see "St Andrew's Park" below).

Yarmouth Way was closed in 1801. Within a few years, a single-storey, flint and brick double cottage (the predecessor of Nos. 209 and 211 Yarmouth Road) and farm buildings had been built across where Mousehold Heath had met Yarmouth Road. The Griffin moved to its present site in 1846, having previously been situated east of St Andrew's Hospital. The part of Yarmouth Road that continued beyond the Griffin changed to its present route in 1856. The part of Yarmouth Road that came from the west changed to its present route in the 1860s.

Octagon Cottage was last occupied in 1963, after which time it fell into disrepair. By 1987 only part of one wall was standing. Today little, if anything, of the structure remains.

*Plate 32 : On the right, the sign of the Griffin and, beyond that, the nurses' home (now Meadowlands) and the asylum, in about 1915.*

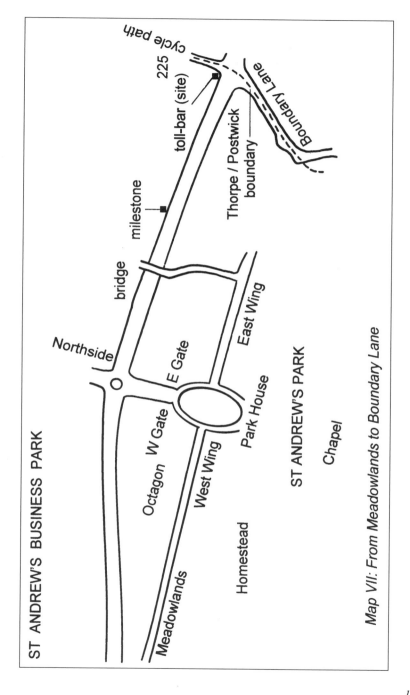

Map VII: From Meadowlands to Boundary Lane

# VII: From Meadowlands to Boundary Lane

## ST ANDREW'S BUSINESS PARK
### FORMERLY PART OF ST ANDREW'S HOSPITAL

East of West Farm, on the north side of the road, was a large enclosed field known in 1589 as "Readings Close" (Plate 38) and owned by Edward Paston, lord of the manor of Thorpe. The name suggests the field was taken in from woodland. The field extended almost as far east as the parish boundary. Part of the field "moved" to the other side of the road when Yarmouth Road was moved northwards in the 1850s. At the same time what was left of the field, and fields to the north, became the asylum farm. The area now forms part of St Andrew's Business Park.

North of what was Readings Close and at the end of what is now Northside were the buildings that were formerly the northern annex of St Andrew's Hospital (previously the County Lunatic Asylum) – see "St Andrew's Park" below. The south-western half of the annex stood on land that before 1801 had been part of Mousehold Heath. The north-eastern half of the annex stood on land that had been part of a large tract of pasture called the Doles that belonged to the manor of Postwick. The annex was built in 1880 and extended in 1903. Many of the buildings are now being demolished to make way for office development. Some of the bricks of the demolished buildings had graffiti etched on them by casualties treated there during the First and Second World Wars. Several of these bricks have been put into storage by Thorpe St Andrew Town Council.

# ST ANDREW'S PARK
## FORMERLY ST ANDREW'S HOSPITAL AND PREVIOUSLY THE COUNTY LUNATIC ASYLUM

## Description

On the south side of the road is what is now called St Andrew's Park. The recent redevelopment of this site as a residential area has included refurbishment of many of the buildings that were part of the 19<sup>th</sup> century asylum.

The "East Gate" and "West Gate" were lodges on either side of the asylum entrance. They were built in 1867. One was used as the doctor's stable.

West of the West Gate, "The Octagon" dates from about 1900. Since it was next to, and provided workers for, the laundry, it was originally called "Laundry Ward". Later it became a recreational and entertainment centre. In 1974 it was named the Octagon Centre after Octagon Cottage (see "Nos. 205 and 207 Yarmouth Road etc" above).

South of East Gate and West Gate are the main surviving buildings.

What are now Nos. 1-18 Park House, Nos. 12-13 East Wing and Nos. 8-9 West Wing was the original asylum of 1812-1814, although with later modifications. For example, the south side of the central section was modified in the late 1870s.

The southern halves of the cross-wings date from about 1830, although they may have been modified in 1842. (They are now No. 14 East Wing and No. 10 West Wing). When they were built, they extended further southwards than now. The northern halves of the cross-wings date from 1842. (They are now Nos. 9-11 East Wing and Nos. 5-7 West Wing). Their northern ends abutted on what was then Yarmouth Road.

*Plate 33 : The asylum from a drawing by J B Ladbrooke of about 1825.*

The lateral extensions at the northern ends of the cross-wings date from the late 1850s, although they have been modified. (They are now Nos. 2-8 East Wing and Nos. 1-4 West Wing). No. 15 East Wing and No. 11 West Wing appear to date from about 1880, although the former is on the site of a part of the building that was erected in 1842 and the latter is on the site of part of the building that was erected in 1830.

West of the West Wing "The Homestead" dates from about 1880. Some of the wards were formerly located there.

South of the main buildings is the asylum chapel, now converted into two dwellings. The octagonal part of it and the bell-tower date from the late 1850s. The nave that adjoins it was added in about 1880. East of the chapel and south of No. 14 East Wing, there was a burial ground that was in use from 1814 until 1858.

### History

In 1810 the Norfolk justices decided to erect a new asylum in Norfolk. Five acres of freehold land in Thorpe were purchased at a cost of £600. Designs were submitted in competition. Francis Stone, the county surveyor, was asked to incorporate the best features from two successful entries, submitted by William Browne of Ipswich and Good and Lockaby of Hatton Gardens. Building work began early in 1812 and, in May 1814, according to the Norfolk Chronicle, "Thorpe asylum was opened for the reception of forty male pauper lunatics." A few months later, female patients were admitted.

The asylum was built to accommodate 100 patients. It consisted of a central three-storey block for the officers and for administrative purposes, with two-storey wings extending east and west. The eastern wing was for female patients and the western wing was for the men.

Thomson, who wrote a brief history in 1903, described the original asylum thus:

> There was a 12 feet (3.5 metres) to 15 feet (4.5 metres) wall round the whole building. The few windows there were, were all iron-barred and grilled. The dormitories and single rooms were called cells. They were almost dark, paved with stone with a drain gulley in the middle of the floor, lighted at night by lanterns in which fish oil was burnt. What little heavy furniture there was, was fixed to the floor. The bedding was a litter of straw on which the inmates lay chained ... The cutlery was of wood or bone and there were tin mugs and platters.

The 1825 river map shows a walled courtyard behind the asylum with a few small buildings outside that. Chambers, in 1829, described it as:

> a noble erection of white [sic] brick, the extent of front being no less than 430 feet (131 metres), with a portico in the centre, supported by four columns. The lowest apartments, or cellars, are covered with a circular vaulting, which sustains the rest of the building. The stone staircase is particularly worthy of notice, from the lightness and strength of its construction; it is of the well form and lighted at the top with a lantern.

There is an engraving of a J B Ladbrooke drawing of the asylum that was published in 1825 (Plate 33). It shows a Classical front with a seven-bay, three-storey centre block with the central three bays projecting under a pediment, with a portico. On either side of the centre block there was a two-storey wing of 16 bays, some projecting. (Apart from one bay at either end, the frontage of the building survives intact as "Park House" – see "Description" above). Not far from the front of the building was a wall with railings that separated the asylum from the road. The engraving shows how close to the building Yarmouth Road used to be.

In 1831 the asylum was enlarged to accommodate 25 more patients on both the male and female sides. The 1841 tithe map shows that this was done by building extensions and southern cross-wings at the eastern and western ends. By 1841 there was a range of buildings south of the male side of the asylum and the same on the female side, including a wash-house and a chapel.

In 1841 it was reported that the asylum was overcrowded, especially on the female (eastern) side. This led to further extensions of the buildings that were completed in 1842. According to White's Norfolk

*Plate 34 : The asylum in about 1905.*

of 1845, the asylum had accommodation for "more than 200 patients, of whom it has generally upwards of 150, who are maintained at the average weekly cost of 5s 9½d per head for the pauper lunatics and 10s for boarders".

It is clear from a plan of January 1854 that the 1842 changes involved modification of the cross-wings. They were extended northwards so their northern ends abutted on what was then Yarmouth Road. The 1854 plan shows that, by that date, south of the central section of the main building was a chapel. This appears to have been partly under the nave and partly under the chancel of the later chapel. South of the eastern wing of the main building was a drying ground. South of the eastern cross-wing was a burial ground.

In 1844 three acres were purchased on the western side of the asylum. Two years later, in 1846, 2.5 acres were acquired on the eastern side of the asylum. The latter included the site of the early 19th century Griffin public house. This was then pulled down and rebuilt in its present location west of the asylum. By early 1854 the newly acquired land had become a garden for the male patients on the western side of the asylum and a recreation area and a garden for the women on the eastern side of the building.

Steadily growing numbers of patients at the asylum meant increasing demand for space. In July 1852 plans for extending the wings of the asylum were approved provided additional space could be obtained for the exercise and employment of patients. In 1853 30 acres were purchased on the north side of Yarmouth Road - from just west of where Northside now is to Green Lane South. (The latter used to continue southwards to what is now the southern end of Old Chapel Way). A similar amount of land west of Northside was leased from the Earl of Rosebery. The new land was used as an asylum farm, where patients were employed.

In the 1852 plans for extending the asylum, it was proposed to provide additional accommodation for 139 patients, a new chapel, a new laundry and drying houses with requisite apparatus. The plans included a new system to supply sufficient water, a new drainage system, apparatus for warming, ventilating and lighting and a dining room "of ample dimensions".

It was not possible to expand southwards because of the common and the unsuitable ground. To expand northwards, the road would have to be moved. Before the enlargement scheme could be approved, a diversion of Yarmouth Road had to be agreed. In January 1854 it was proposed to divert Yarmouth Road so that it ran to the south of the hospital. The turnpike trustees rejected this, because it would mean a longer road and a steep ascent at the western end. It would also interfere with the consecrated burial ground at the asylum. In March 1854 a proposal to divert the turnpike to the north of the asylum was accepted provided the diversion continued further at the western end than had been suggested.

Work on the new road was completed in 1856. At its furthest point

*Plate 35 : Norfolk War Hospital in about 1915.*

the new road was 100 yards (91 metres) from the front of the hospital. The old road had been 30 yards (27 metres) away. The excavated earth formed fortification-like mounds in front of the asylum. Also, in 1856, a new permanent bridge was built across the road "for the convenience of the workmen on the farm". The bridge still exists, having replaced a temporary footbridge over the road that was built in 1855.

About 40 yards (37 metres) east of the bridge, there is a milestone against the wall on the north side of the road. Presumably this also dates from 1856, although it may have been moved from the old road. It records the fact that it is three miles from Norwich and 19 miles from Yarmouth.

As the new road was completed, work on the new asylum buildings began. A new laundry, east and west towers for water storage in case of fire, and new workshops were built between the new road and what had been the old road. Near the east tower, a slaughter-house was built. Next door to it was a building where vegetables were cooked. Just east of the bridge across from the farm, there was a reservoir. New blocks of wards were added by lateral extensions at the northern ends of the cross-wings of the main asylum building. South of it an octagonal chapel with a bell-tower was built and a new dining-hall was erected.

In the 1860s and 1870s further changes were made. In 1861 farm buildings were erected on the asylum's land to the north of the road. The lodges at the entrance to the asylum were added in 1867 (Plate 34). Extra wards were added to the female side of the asylum in 1869 and 1873. Two wards on the male side were extended in 1876.

Thomson records that:

in 1880, further additions to the existing buildings being impossible, the committee decided to build an Annex or Auxiliary Asylum on land to the north of the Main Asylum, about 500 yards (457 metres) away. The Annex would be a plain, simple and comparatively cheap building to house quiet and tractable chronic cases. It would contain 280 beds, 140 of each sex.

The original asylum was in yellow brick and the extensions to it in "white" brick. It was decided that the new asylum should be in red brick. According to White's Norfolk of 1883, the new building was "after the design of R M Phipson of Norwich" and consisted of "two large wards for males and females, with dormitories, baths and all requisites… The airing court or garden where the patients take recreation comprises an acre and a half of ground, tastefully laid out with flowerbeds, shrubs, drinking fountains etc."

Also in 1880, a nave was added to the octagonal chapel at the old asylum.

Between 1885 and 1912 accommodation was built for staff outside the asylums. In the 1880s and 1890s a row of eighteen attendants' cottages was erected on the north side of Yarmouth Road, next to the Thorpe boundary, but just into Postwick. They were known as the "Norfolk Cottages". They were demolished in 1997. In 1892 a large house was built for the medical superintendent. This was also on the north side of Yarmouth Road, but just within Thorpe. Until 1892, the superintendent had been housed in uncomfortable and inadequate quarters in the centre of the old asylum. His new house was known as "Thorpe End". It was pulled down in the 1990s.

There were major changes at the asylum in 1903. The main purpose was to provide extra accommodation for the male patients. The old asylum would now just be for female patients and the new asylum just for men. The changes included building a road to the new asylum (now Northside) and increasing accommodation there by constructing a large south-west extension. The whole asylum would contain 1000 beds – 550 at the old or women's asylum and 450 at the new or men's asylum.

At the old asylum, a new boiler house and central generating station was built on the eastern side, including subways for water mains. Work included the construction of a chimney, 110 feet high (33.5 metres), next to the boiler house. The chimney was demolished in 1977.

A 1903 description of the old or women's asylum describes what the complex was like. The central administrative block consisted of a board room where the monthly meetings of the committees were held, offices for the medical superintendent, the clerk and the steward, quarters and mess for the assistant medical officers and matrons, a dispensary, steward's stores, and visiting room. Buildings stretching east and west consisted of wards, laundry, kitchens, chapel, recreation hall, nurses' mess rooms and bedrooms, fire station, engineer's and clerk of works' departments, stables and coach-houses, and the sewage works.

In 1910 a nurses' home for 50 nurses was built on the western side of the old asylum, near the Griffin (Plate 32). The building is now known as Meadowlands. In 1912 a new recreation hall was erected south-east of the central administrative block.

In April 1915 the asylum was converted into a military hospital – the Norfolk War Hospital (Plate 35). Repeated extensions of the hospital buildings became necessary, and the institution came to contain about 2,450 beds for sick and wounded soldiers. There were three divisions – the main hospital, the annex hospital and the camp (situated behind the annex). Thorpe Hospital was the central hospital in Norfolk to the fifty auxiliary (or VAD) hospitals scattered throughout the county. It was officially closed in April 1919. In 1920 Earl Haig unveiled a plaque in the entrance hall of the hospital, recording that 45,000 military patients had been treated there between 1915 and 1919.

In 1920 the asylum changed its name to the Norfolk Mental Hospital and in 1925 the name changed again to St Andrew's Hospital.

During the Second World War evacuee, military and civilian casualties were treated in the northern annex.

The hospital closed in the summer of 1998. The north-western quarter of the site has been redeveloped as St. Andrew's Business Park and the north-eastern quarter as Bannatyne's Health Club and the western edge of Broadland Business Park. The southern side of the site has been turned into a prestigious housing development, St Andrew's Park.

# DUSSINDALE

North of Sainsbury's, between Pound Lane and the railway line, is a modern housing development called Dussindale Park. It is named after the site of the final battle of Kett's rebellion on Tuesday 27th August 1549 when the rebels were defeated. What is the evidence for Dussindale and where did the battle take place?

## The location of Dussindale

In 2002, in the first edition of this history, it was argued that Dussindale might be the valley that runs west along Valley Drive, off Heartsease Lane. It runs north across Gurney Road and then west through Long Valley to Gilman Road. It was pointed out that, in about 1720, Kirkpatrick drew a plan of the earthworks of St William's chapel, Mousehold Heath, between Mousehold Lane and Gurney Road. He annotated the plan with notes, including a statement that the chapel was about 260 paces north of Dussindale (Dussyns Dale). Since he said that ten of his paces equalled about nine yards (eight metres), it meant Dussindale was about 234 yards (214 metres) south of the chapel site. This takes you to just north of where Valley Drive joins Gurney Road.

Kirkpatrick did not say why he believed the Valley Drive site was Dussindale. There are no other documentary references to it. It may be that an artefact or skeleton had been found there and so it had been assumed this was the site of the battle. In the mid-late 19th century a worker in a brick pit in a valley running down to Long Valley is said to have come across so many skeletons in the brick-earth they were digging that they had to stop and backfill the ground. The story comes from someone who heard it from a heath ranger who had heard it in the 1930s from the grandson of the person who claimed to have made the discovery.

However, the weight of the argument rests with the view, first put forward by Anne Carter in 1984, that Dussindale was situated on the boundary between the parishes of Thorpe St Andrew and Postwick and Thorpe St Andrew and Great Plumstead. Having examined the evidence, some modification is necessary, as it appears that at Brook Farm (now the northernmost part of Pym Close) Dussindale turned westwards and then west-north-westwards and continued nearly as far as the boundary with Sprowston. This seems to be why the 1549 indictment against Kett said that the rebels were defeated at Dussindale ("Dussingesdale") in "the parishes of Thorpe and Sprowston".

According to a river survey of 1767, the stream that ran through the valley was called the Muck Fleet. Bryant says that in 1593 it was known as the Muckeflete. It is clearly shown on Faden's map of the early 1790s. It is highly likely that the whole of the shallow valley down which this stream flowed was called Dussindale. However, apart from the indictment against Kett, the documentary references to Dussindale all relate to the part of the valley south of Brook Farm or rather south of the eastern third of Great Lumners Close (Plate 36). Brook Farm was at the eastern end of this close. In 1735 Thomas Harrison described the most southern part of the valley near Thorpe Common as Dussindale. The part south of the eastern third of Great Lumners Close is called Dussindale on the 1718 map. Today this last reference means south of the building known as No. 1 Brook Road, which is just north of the Norvic Centre and what used to be the northern annex of St Andrew's Hospital. There are several references to Dussindale in the 1576 field book for the manor of Postwick and Great Plumstead. In addition, Dussindale is referred to in a description of the boundaries of the foldcourses of Lumners and Great Plumstead in a lease from the Cathedral Priory dated 10th March 1535.

Just before it entered the Yare, the Muck Fleet flowed across Thorpe Common along the boundary ditch between Thorpe and Postwick. Harrison said the valley ran up from the "nook of the East part of Thorp Comon directly towards Drove Lane" which was "the Bottom of the Valley called Dussings Dale". What this means is that before running under Yarmouth Road, the Muck Fleet ran along the parish boundary with Postwick next to a drove road (referred to on the 1589 Mousehold map as "Poswick Townes Droveway unto Mushold"). The drove road entered Mousehold Heath at the northern boundary of Readings Close (Plate 38). This is now near the western end of a building called Lakeside 500, at the end of Old Chapel Way.

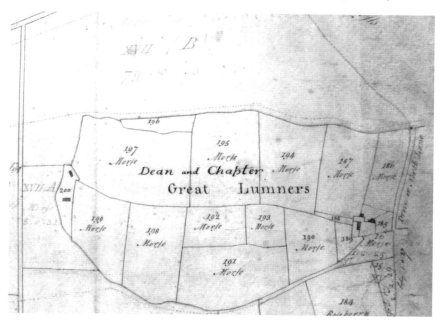

*Plate 36: Great Lumners Close and the junction between the proposed Plumstead Road East and Pound Lane, from the 1800 enclosure map. At the eastern end of Great Lumners Close was Brook Farm.*

If Faden's map is reinterpreted in the light of the Ordnance Survey, it shows that the valley through which the river ran continued northwards through a sheep-pasture or bruery called the Doles. The middle of the valley continued to run along the Thorpe / Postwick boundary. The Doles stretched as far west as the eastern boundary of Mousehold Heath (referred to on the 1718 map as "The Great Old Dyke"). They appear to have been partly in Thorpe and partly in Postwick, although until at least the 18th century, Postwick claimed they were all in Postwick, and that the Mousehold boundary was the parish boundary. The 1718 map marks the section of the valley that ran through the

Doles as "Dussings Deale and Poswick Sheeps Walk". "Poswick Sheeps Walk" was an alternative name for the Doles.

North of the Doles the centre of the valley ran along the parish boundary between Thorpe and Great Plumstead. To the west were closes called Little Lumners. Although they were in Thorpe, they belonged to the lord of the manor of Great Plumstead. To the east was Great Plumstead Common also known as the Smee. This was north of what is now Smee Lane.

It is clear that at Brook Farm the valley turned westwards and bisected Great Lumners Close. The 1880s Ordnance Survey map (Plate 37) shows a track running along the bottom of the valley just north of The Woodlands. Today the valley can be seen as a dip in Dussindale Drive near its junction with Fiennes Road. It continued until the beginning of what is now Brown's Plantation, where it headed west-north-westwards as far as Plumstead Road East. It was still in Thorpe but not far from the Sprowston border. It was in what is now Belmore Plantation, and reached Plumstead Road East almost midway between South Hill Road and Pound Lane.

In modern terms, this suggests that Dussindale includes Broadland Business Park nearly as far as the eastern north-south arm of Peachman Way and Broadland Way. A better limit would have been the old Green Lane South that ran from what is now the Smee Lane roundabout south-south-westwards to the southern end of Old Chapel Way. It also includes the north-eastern halves of the Norvic Clinic and what was formerly the northern annex of St Andrew's Hospital. In addition, it includes land to the north between the railway line and Green Lane. On the western side of the railway line, it includes the part of the Dussindale housing development between the railway line and an imaginary line running north-east approximately from where Dalbier Close meets Desborough Way to the Green Lane North railway bridge. In addition, it includes the part of the housing development north of this line or north of a line west from where Dalbier Close meets Desborough

Way to the western end of Montrose Close (together these two areas equate with the southern half of Great Lumners Close). It also includes the field to the north of the housing development (this equates with the northern half of Great Lumners Close). In addition, it includes the Oasis Sports and Leisure Club (Pound Lane) and woodland on either side of Pound Lane called Brown's Plantation and Belmore Plantation (both south of Plumstead Road East and containing ponds).

Sotherton's contemporary account of the battle says "Dussens Dale" was "not past a myle of[f] and somewhat more" from the rebels' camp. Although the rebels' headquarters were at the top of Gas Hill, there is a hint that the camp extended as far east as Harvey Lane. The Norwich Chamberlains accounts of 1549 refer to the rebels being "Inkennelled on Mushold hethe and in thorpe wood". The eastern boundary of "thorpe wood" was Harvey Lane (see "Harvey Lane" above). Belmore Plantation is about a mile from the top of Harvey Lane, whereas the bottom of Dussindale on Yarmouth Road is just under two miles from the bottom of Harvey Lane. This might explain the rather confusing reference to how far away Dussindale was.

**The site of the battle**

The evidence quoted identifies the location of Dussindale rather than the exact site of the battle. The best evidence for the Dussindale place-name is south of No. 1 Brook Road, east of the railway line. However, as explained above, it is clear that after Brook Farm, the valley extended westwards and then west-north-westwards as far as Plumstead Road East (Plate 37). It is this northern section in the region of what is now Brown's Plantation and Belmore Plantation that is nearest to the Sprowston border. This is important because, as mentioned above, there is a contemporary reference to the rebels' defeat at Dussindale taking place in Thorpe and Sprowston, which suggests the area of the border between the two parishes. The region of Brown's and Belmore Plantations was also an unenclosed part of Mousehold Heath and on a direct route, along Plumstead Road East, from the rebels' camp. These factors make it a good candidate for the battle site.

The rebels would have known the value of high ground. In the Duke of Somerset's letter of 1 September 1549 to the Ambassador Sir Philip Hoby, he said of the rebels, "issuing out of their campe into a plaine nere adjoyning, thei determinede to fight". This reference to a plain suggests the battle took place on the generally flat land on the top of Mousehold Heath rather than in the Yare valley.

In describing preparations for the battle, Blomefield said the rebels "threw a ditch cross the high ways". In this area, near the border between Thorpe and Sprowston, a number of east-west roads crossed the heath quite close to each other. From north to south, they were St Benets Way (which in part followed the border with Sprowston), Ranworth Way, Walsham Way (now Plumstead Road East) and Rampes Lane (Plate 37 - see also "Roads" in Appendix 2 below). It is likely that the rebels blocked some or all of them.

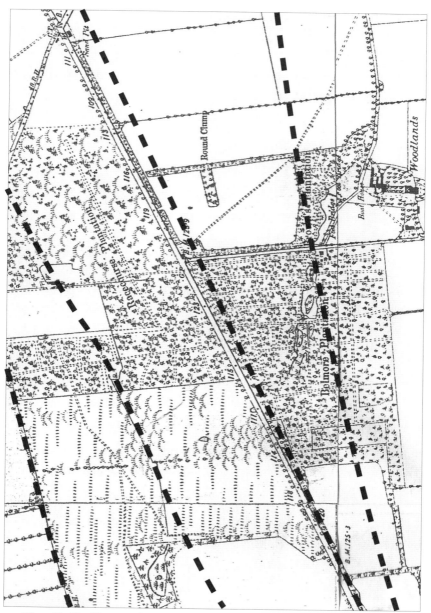

*Plate 37: The Plumstead Road East / Pound Lane junction area from the 1880s Ordnance Survey map, showing approximate routes of pre-1801 roads that from north to south are St Benets Way, Ranworth Way, Walsham Way and Rampes Lane.*

# NUMBER 225 YARMOUTH ROAD, THE SITE OF THE TOLL-BAR AND THE PARISH BOUNDARY

The last house in Thorpe is No. 225 Yarmouth Road. South of this, by the roadside, until the 1960s, there was a house called "Sunflower Cottage". It was reconstructed and re-roofed in 1900, when it was the house of the resident engineer to the asylum (see "St Andrew's Park" above). Before it was largely rebuilt, it was a mid-19th century cottage that in 1888 was referred to as "Old Tollgate House". From 1769 until about 1840, it was here at the boundary between Thorpe and Postwick that there was a toll-bar across the road, known as Postwick Gate. It is marked on the 1800 enclosure map (Plate 38).

In about 1840 it was replaced by a tollgate at the western extremity of Thorpe. The latter went across from what is now the Canton Chinese Restaurant, No. 129 Thorpe Road, but was previously the Redan. It was called the Thorpe Gate and remained in use until 1874, when tolls were abolished, the toll-house was demolished and the Redan public house was built on the site. Midway between what was the Redan and Telegraph Lane East, on the north side of the road, there used to be milestone that was one mile from Norwich and 21 miles from Yarmouth.

East of No. 225 Yarmouth Road there is a cycle path that initially follows what was the northern side of Boundary Lane, the parish boundary between Thorpe and Postwick. As mentioned in "Dussindale" above, between here and what used to be Brook Farm (now the northernmost part of Pym Close), the parish boundary followed a stream called the Muck Fleet that ran down a valley called Dussindale. Today, going northwards, the parish boundary is picked up by the western north-south arm of Peachman Way and Brook Road. It then follows the line of Brook Road northwards to where a railway bridge crosses Green Lane North. This is close to the site of Brook Farm.

Brook Farm was at the eastern end of a close called Great Lumners Close (Plate 36). This, and an attaching foldcourse on Mousehold

Heath, were leased from Norwich Cathedral as part of an estate called Lumners that used to belong to the Cathedral Priory (see Appendix 2, "Sheep", below). The farm buildings were demolished in about 1997 to make way for an extension to the Dussindale housing development. They are now the northernmost part of Pym Close.

North of the Green Lane North railway bridge, Thorpe's eastern boundary is with Great Plumstead. Here the boundary follows the line of Green Lane North up to the junction with Plumstead Road East. The section of Green Lane North between the railway bridge and the junction with Middle Road followed the eastern boundary of Great Lumners Close and was called Drove Lane in 1589, Lumners Lane in 1718 and Drove or North Lane in 1800. Until 1801, the junction with Middle Road was where the parish boundary began to cross Mousehold Heath. Today, where Green Lane North meets Plumstead Road East, the parish boundary crosses that road and continues north-westwards between the western edge of the Heath Road development and Racecourse Plantation until it meets the boundary with Sprowston.

On the south side of Yarmouth Road, the boundary goes south-westwards along part of Boundary Lane and then continues south-south-westwards along a ditch to the river.

*Plate 38: The eastern end of Thorpe from the 1800 enclosure map. 180 and 179 were previously one field called Readings Close.*

# Appendix 1 Thorpe Manor

## *Lordship of the manor until 1535*

The first-recorded lord of the manor of Thorpe was Stigand who was head of Edward the Confessor's secretariat and bishop of East Anglia in 1042. Stigand was probably granted Thorpe by Edward the Confessor in 1042, although he may have received it earlier since he had been an influential royal adviser since at least 1020, when he was priest to King Cnut. According to the Anglo-Saxon Chronicle, in 1043, Edward turned against his mother, Emma, and against Stigand, his mother's "closest confidant" and adviser. Stigand lost his bishopric and lands, but they were restored to him later that year. He held the bishopric until 1047 and lands (including Thorpe) until 1070, when he fell from favour and William I confiscated his property. Stigand was archbishop of Canterbury from 1052 until 1070 and as such appears in the Bayeux Tapestry at the coronation of King Harold in 1066.

Thorpe may be an early royal manor. There is support for this from place-name evidence. Bishopgate leads to Bishop Bridge, the lowest fording point on the Wensum and probably where a Roman road crossed the river on its way to Brundall. Ayers has suggested that within the Cathedral Close and near the river-crossing was the site of a small Middle Saxon settlement (probably of the $8^{th}$ century) which can be identified with the place-name "Conesford", meaning King's ford, because it led to the King's manor of Thorpe. The reference in the Domesday Book to "woodland for 1200 pigs" suggests that Thorpe had the largest wood in Norfolk. According to Williamson, "most of the largest totals of woodland were attached to places which had been ancient estate centres, especially those which had remained in royal hands" and/or were the centres of hundreds. Since there is no evidence of Thorpe being the centre of a hundred, the size of the wood supports the idea that it was the ancient centre of a royal estate.

Of the 11 villages that surrounded Mousehold before it was enclosed in 1801, Thorpe is the only village whose Domesday Book entry mentions significant woodland. No other Mousehold parish seems to have had woodland for more than 15 pigs. The disparity between Thorpe and the other Mousehold parishes may suggest that the Thorpe part of Mousehold had received some special, perhaps royal, protection which had stopped it turning into a treeless heath.

After Stigand lost the manor of Thorpe in 1070, William I granted it to Earl Ralph de Guader. In 1075 the manor passed back to the king, as a result of the earl's rebellion. It remained in the hands of the Crown until 1101 when Henry I granted it to Herbert de Losinga, bishop of Norwich.

## Lordship of the manor from 1535

By an Act of Parliament passed in February 1535, Henry VIII seized most of the lands of the bishop of Norwich (including Thorpe) and granted him in exchange the estates of St Benet's abbey.

In 1544 Henry granted the manor of Thorpe to Thomas, Duke of Norfolk with remainder to his son Henry, Earl of Surrey. Two years earlier, Surrey had obtained a lease of St Leonard's Priory, which he was pulling down and replacing with a great house that became known as Mount Surrey. The acquisition of the manor of Thorpe was probably regarded as a logical extension of this endeavour. However, three years after acquiring Thorpe, the Duke of Norfolk and the Earl of Surrey were convicted of treason. Their property passed to the Crown. Surrey was executed.

In July 1547 Henry granted the manor of Thorpe to Sir Thomas Paston, a member of the king's Privy Chamber. Sir Thomas had married Agnes, daughter and heiress of Sir John Leigh of Addington, Surrey. When Sir Thomas died, in 1550, Thorpe passed to his son Edward, who was then just a few months old. Edward attained age 21 in 1571. By his second wife, Margaret, daughter of Henry Berney of Reedham,

Edward had six sons and three daughters. In 1608 Edward's eldest son, Thomas, married Mary, daughter of Sir George Browne, the second son of Viscount Montague. Under the terms of a settlement, Edward agreed that Thorpe (with Paston and Blofield, several marshes and other property in Norfolk and Suffolk) would pass to Thomas on Edward's death. Edward also settled Binham and Barney on Thomas and Mary. Thomas died in 1622, eight years before his father. Edward died in 1630 and was remembered on his tablet in Blofield church as "most skillfull of liberal sciences especially musicke and poetry as also strange languages". Under the settlement, the manor then passed to Edward's grandson, Clement, who was then under 21. Clement, like his grandfather, was a Catholic. As a result, when the Civil War began in 1642, Clement's land was sequestered which meant that all income and profits went to Parliament and its soldiers. Thorpe was released from sequestration in 1656 and Clement sold the manor to the Reverend Nathan Wright, a Norwich prebend. Clement died in 1662.

By 1670 the manor was in the hands of Rowland Dee, a London merchant. In 1720 his son's widow sold it to Matthew Howard, another London merchant. He died in 1737 and in 1751 his two daughters sold the manor to Thomas Vere, a worsted manufacturer who was mayor of Norwich in 1735 and an MP for Norwich from 1735 until 1747. On Thomas' death in 1766, the manor passed to his son John Vere. In 1790 John Vere died without children and, under the terms of his father's will, the manor passed to his father's "much Esteemed Friend", Thomas Lobb Chute of South Pickenham. Nine months later, in November 1790, Thomas Lobb Chute died. The manor then passed to his son, the Reverend Thomas Vere Chute of the Vyne, Hampshire.

Between 1802 and 1803 Thomas Vere Chute sold off the estate attached to the manor and Sir Roger Kerrison bought most of it. Chute retained the lordship of the manor. When he died, in 1827, William Lyde Wiggett succeeded him and changed his name to Wiggett Chute. He was the second son of Chute's cousin, the Reverend James Wiggett. In 1836 the lordship of the manor passed to James Cuddon, who died in 1851. In 1861 it passed from the Cuddon family to William Birkbeck. On his death in 1897, he was succeeded by his son William John Birkbeck. He died in 1916, whereupon the manor passed to the trustees of his will.

# Appendix 2 - Mousehold Heath and Thorpe Wood

Mousehold Heath was an ancient wood-pasture that stretched from Norwich north-eastwards as far as Woodbastwick and Ranworth. In the 13th century it was known as Musholt, which means "mouse-infested wood". The part of it that lay within Thorpe was known as Thorpe Wood. In the 12th century Thorpe Wood was held in common between the bishop of Norwich and the Cathedral Priory. This led to disputes and so, in 1239, it was agreed that Thorpe Wood should be physically divided between them. However, it is far from certain how much of this agreement was implemented.

What is clear from the 1239 agreement is that by that time Thorpe Wood had two distinct areas. There was (1) the part covered with oaks and (2) the part covered with holly-wood and heathland.

## *The oak wood (now Lion Wood)*

The part of Thorpe Wood covered with oaks is the origin of what is today called Lion Wood and lies to the west of Harvey Lane. Rather confusingly, a draft Norwich charter of 1461 and the Norwich charter of 1556 refer to it as Thorpe Wood. In the 13th century it covered 155 acres. In 1239 it was agreed that it be divided into two equal parts, but it is clear from a 16th century lease that this never happened. By 1589 the wood was only about 100 acres and was between (1) Heathside Road and an imaginary line continuing northwards as far as what is now the waterworks tower and (2) Harvey Lane from the bottom up as far as Rockland Drive. In the 16th century it was known as the "partible woode of Thorp". By 1589 the Dean and Chapter (the successor to the Cathedral Priory) had given up their legal interest in it to Edward Paston (the successor as lord of the manor to the bishop of Norwich). Between 1800 and 1818 John Harvey (see "Thorpe Lodge" above) reduced the area of woodland from 61 acres to 21 acres. The current Lion Wood covers about 23 acres. The track that runs between Wellesley Avenue South and Wellesley Avenue North is an important dividing line. To the east is part of what in 1800 was known as Layne Wood (by 1819 known as Lion Wood). To the west are parts of what in 1800 were known as Thorofare Wood and Hill Wood. These were the two woods that Harvey cut down completely. He also reduced Layne Wood by about 5.5 acres.

## *The holly-wood and heathland*

The part of Thorpe Wood covered with holly-wood and heathland is the origin of what is today called Mousehold Heath. The official boundary of today's Mousehold Heath only encompasses 184 acres. The Thorpe-next-Norwich Enclosure Act 1800 resulted in the enclosure of 1,377 acres of heathland in Thorpe that had been part of Mousehold. It did not affect the present Mousehold Heath, as this was not regarded as part of Thorpe. It would be correct to call it Pockthorpe Heath, as it was within the extramural parish of Pockthorpe (also known as the parish of St Catherine), which, in about 1410, amalgamated with the intramural parish of St James. Medieval documents (including the 1239 agreement) suggest that Pockthorpe extended as far south as Gas Hill / Yarmouth Way and as far east as the 15th/16th century Norwich boundary. (This eastern boundary may have derived from the 1239 division of the heath between the bishop of Norwich and the Cathedral Priory). However, from the 16th to the 18th century Thorpe claimed that what could be called Pockthorpe Heath was within their parish. The matter was settled in 1800 when the Enclosure Commissioners satisfied themselves that Pockthorpe extended as far east as the Norwich boundary and as far south as Beech Drive, the current official southern boundary of Mousehold Heath.

The 1800 Enclosure Act related to both the city and the county sides of Thorpe. What follows concentrates on the county side i.e. the modern Thorpe St Andrew. In 1800 just over 50% of Thorpe St Andrew, namely the northern half, was Mousehold Heath. So the turning of this heathland into fields was a major change. The 1600 Mousehold map and records relating to a late 16th century court case

(Tenants of South Walsham v Edward Paston and Miles Corbet) and the 1800/1801 enclosure of Thorpe show how Mousehold Heath was used before 1801.

## Sheep

Under the East Anglian foldcourse system, sheep grazed on heathland from 25th March to 29th September, while crops were growing in the open arable fields. In 1800 the lord of the manor of Thorpe had a right of sheep walk (i.e. to graze sheep) over Thorpe Fouldcourse for 450 sheep - 338 ewes and their followers and 112 wethers (a wether is a castrated male sheep). It appears from the 1600 Mousehold map that Thorpe Fouldcourse was between the city boundary on the west and the banked boundary of Lumners Fouldcourse on the east. Faden's map of the 1790s shows a "Shepherd's House" on the heath, on the south side of Plumstead Road East just east of the Heartsease Lane roundabout. It's likely that it related to Thorpe Fouldcourse.

In 1800 the Dean and Chapter (through their lessee John Morse junior) had grazing rights over Lumners Fouldcourse for 280 sheep. This foldcourse covered 325 acres and was part of a Dean and Chapter (previously Cathedral Priory) estate, referred to in the 15th century as Lomnours. The foldcourse was to the north, west and south-west of an 86 acre close called Great Lumners (or Lomners) (Plate 36). By about 1700, at the western end of the close was a shepherd's house and at the eastern end a farm that was later called Brook Farm. The farm was very close to the parish boundary between Thorpe and Great Plumstead.

The 1800 enclosure map shows the boundary bank between Thorpe Fouldcourse and Lumners Fouldcourse. It ran south-eastwards from the parish boundary with Sprowston (the ends of the gardens on the south side of Greenborough Road) and through what is now Racecourse Plantation, passing just west of the pond that is north-east of Paston Way. (The pond is marked on the 1600 Mousehold map). The bank crossed Plumstead Road East near its present junction with South Hill Road and crossed Pound Lane about 180 yards (165 metres) north of its junction with Laundry Lane. It continued as far as the northern boundary of Garget Hills, which it would have reached near the western end of the east-west stretch of Naseby Way. These banks (and also the banks on the border with Mousehold) would have gone by 1801; no trace of them can be seen today.

## *Tenants' rights to grazing and fuel*

Although the lord of the manor had the exclusive right to pasture sheep on Thorpe Fouldcourse, the tenants, by virtue of their land-holdings, had the right to graze their "great cattle" (i.e. horses, cows, bulls and oxen) on the heath. In 1800 this right was claimed by almost all of the 29 landowners.

Some tenants, also by virtue of their land-holdings, had the right "to grave, dig and make flaggs and to fell and take all manner of ling and braks growing thereon for their own use and to sell to others". This means they could dig up fibrous subsurface material and make dried blocks (flags) of low quality fuel. They could also cut down the heather (ling) and gorse (bracken or furze). The primary use was for fuel, although heather could be used as low-grade thatch and gorse could be used as litter for livestock. In 1800 this right was claimed by only three of the 29 landowners. This is because the right had been restricted by the granting of doles to particular individuals.

## *Doles*

A dole is a marked-out portion of a heath, common or open field granted by the lord of the manor to a particular tenant for a particular purpose. At Thorpe, on Mousehold Heath, the exclusive right granted related to the "cutting and taking of Flaggs and Lyng." In the 16th century the lord of the manor claimed unsuccessfully that, apart from those with doles, no one had the right to cut and take turf or heather unless the right had been granted by deed or the manor court.

In Thorpe, in 1589, there was a series of six doles along the edge of the heath between approximately what is now Henby Way and "The olde Church pathe" just east of Hilly Plantation. Four of them were east of Thunder Lane (then Drovegate Way) and their northern boundary was Walsham Way (now Plumstead Road East). The other two were east of Thunder Lane. In addition there were doles in the eastern and north-eastern part of the parish. Three were on the eastern boundary of Mousehold between Great Lumners Close and Readings Close and belonged to the lord of the manor of Great Plumstead. Four were around Great Lumners Close. Six were north or north-west of this close, on the edge of a banked area of heathland north of Walsham Way, called Gyddyng heathe (Gilden Heath in 1535) that was mostly within Lumners Fouldcourse.

Some of these doles are among the five mentioned in 1800. One of the two doles east of Thunder Lane was ten acres. A dole near the south-west corner of Gyddyng heathe (Wees Dole) was nearly 81 acres, while another dole was 22 acres.

Mousehold was an important source of fuel for the people of Norwich, but the stripping of the heath meant it couldn't be used for productive agricultural purposes. In 1800 Arthur Young wrote:

> The greatest evil upon Moushold heath is the paring the surface for fuel. This is ruin, and has destroyed that end of the heath which bears towards Norwich. This under any system should be prevented.

## *Brueries*

A bruery was a form of dole where the exclusive right granted related, not to cutting fuel, but to grazing. According to Butcher, a bruery can be "marked out in strips, or fenced off into enclosures, and used for rough grazing". It tended to be land on the edge of a heath that, although remaining part of the heath, was marked out in a special way.

So in 1800 Jehoshaphat Postle had 100 acres of freehold "bruery ground" on the part of the heath called Garget Hills (south of Peddelers Way) and claimed grazing rights in respect of it. (This land seems to have been held by Mr Gybson in 1589). In addition, Isaac Marsh claimed "10 acres of Bruery, or Dole, formerly of Edward Giles, lying upon Mousehold Heath, which is copyhold of the said Manor."

## *Mineral rights*

In 1800 there was only one successful claim for mineral rights over the heath. It was to rights "of digging and taking Marl, Mould, Gravel and Clay."

The 1589 Mousehold map does show pits on the heath. Most are within the city boundary, but outside it were "Cookes pytts", in the angle between St William's Way and Harvey Lane.

## *Roads*

### *East-west roads*

Various east-west roads across the heath were affected by the 1800 enclosure (Plate 37). They are nearly all shown on the 1600 Mousehold map. Some appear on the 1800 enclosure map. Other key maps are the 1589 Mousehold map and the 1718 map.

In 1718 the most northern road was called St Benets Way. Its east-west stretch ran along most of the parish boundary with Sprowston, almost as far as the "Whight Stake", which was where the boundaries of Thorpe, Great Plumstead and Sprowston met. Ranworth Way (1589) ran not far south of St Benets Way. Not far south of Ranworth Way was Walsham Way (1589). To the south was another road called Rampes Lane (1589) or Plumstead Way (1718); its route included the northern boundary of Great Lumners Close (Plate 36). Further south was a road that ran along the heath boundary to Thunder Lane and continued eastwards to the boundary between Postwick and Great Plumstead. In 1589 this road was known as Peddelers Way or Wytton Way. At Thunder Lane a road branched north-eastwards from Peddelers Way to Brook Farm at the eastern end of Great Lumners Close – in 1589 this was called Lomners Lane or Plumsty Way. Further south still was Yarmouth Way (1589).

In 1801 Walsham Way was straightened and became a public road that is now Plumstead Road up to Harvey Lane and then Plumstead Road East. St Benets Way, Ranworth Way, Rampes Lane, Peddelers Way, Lomners Lane and Yarmouth Way were all closed and absorbed into the new fields. A small stretch of Yarmouth Way was set out at enclosure as a private road – now Hilly Plantation, off Thunder Lane.

### North-south roads

Two existing north-south roads were extended across the heath, following in part existing tracks. One new north-south road was constructed.

Harvey Lane (then called Rose or Rose's Lane) was extended northwards from just south of Gordon Avenue. It continued across the new Plumstead Road, where it became part of Heartsease Lane. Harvey Lane ran in a much more northerly direction than the city boundary which went north-north-east and then north-north-west. Thunder Lane (also called Sheeps Path Lane) was extended northwards from just south of Laundry Close. It continued across the new Plumstead Road East, where it became part of Woodside Road. These extensions to Harvey Lane and Thunder Lane were public roads. Pound Lane was constructed up to Plumstead Road East as a completely new private road. A short private road was constructed off Thunder Lane; this equates with Laundry Close.

# *Enclosure*

At Thorpe, there is little evidence of enclosure before the general enclosure of 1800/1801. It appears from the 1589 Mousehold map that Mousehold was bordered generally by a bank with trees on top. However this was not the case with the border with much of Sprowston to the north or Thorpe to the south. The border between Mousehold and Sprowston was Ravensgate Way. In 1589 the border with the part of Thorpe between Harvey Lane and Nos. 205/207 Yarmouth Road was a line of fields immediately north of Yarmouth Way. It is likely that they were taken in from Mousehold, the fields between Harvey Lane and Thunder Lane perhaps by Paston in the middle of the 16th century. This would mean that the earlier boundary with Mousehold was Yarmouth Way.

The Thorpe Enclosure Act was passed in 1800. Enclosure Commissioners were appointed and on 12th April 1800 they gave notice that they would hold their first meeting on 23rd April. On 3rd May they invited anyone claiming an interest in Mousehold Heath to submit an account in writing at their meeting on 26th May. On 28th June anyone with objections to the claims was invited to raise them before 10th July, so they could be considered at a meeting on 21st July.

On 3rd May the Commissioners gave notice in the Norfolk Chronicle and the Norwich Mercury that they would perambulate the boundary of the parish on 27th May. On 6th September they gave notice that they had ascertained, fixed and determined the parish boundary that was then described. It may have been at this point that the Commissioners appointed Robert Chasteney of Trowse to make a survey or plan of the parish. By the end of 1800 he had drawn up a draft map of the whole parish of Thorpe, showing also the proposed new roads and enclosures on Mousehold Heath. This is the map that is referred to in this book as the 1800 enclosure map.

On 14th February 1801 the Commissioners gave notice that the allotments they intended to be make on Mousehold would be ploughed or staked out on or before 23rd February, so the respective proprietors could view them. Any objections to these allotments would be heard at a meeting on 27th February. The Norwich Mercury of 4th April 1801 stated:

> The inclosure of Mousehold Heath, which so long employed the minds of speculative men in calculating its probable advantages, has at length commenced and is rapidly proceeding. We understand that considerable allotments under the Thorpe Bill have been sold for sums, which, on the usual average for computing the value of similar purchases, would amount to an annual rent of 25 shillings per acre.

The final award and division of Mousehold Heath was read and executed at a special meeting of the Commissioners held on 27th July 1801. It included descriptions of the boundaries of the parish and of the new public and private roads that had been set out across Mousehold. It contained a map and description of the allotments of land on the former Mousehold Heath. It referred to certain exchanges of land that would take effect from the date of the award.

The enclosure of the part of Mousehold Heath that was in parish of Thorpe-next-Norwich did not happen in isolation. The Enclosure Act relating to the part of Mousehold that was in Sprowston was also passed in 1800. The Sprowston award was executed on 9th October 1801. An Act relating to Great Plumstead was the last Enclosure Act to be passed in respect of Mousehold Heath, in 1810. The award was executed in 1812.

## *Horse racing*

St Benets Way ran along much of the boundary with Sprowston (see "Roads" above), It ran midway between what is now Salhouse Road and Plumstead Road / Plumstead Road East. The 1718 map shows that part of St Benets Way had become a "raceground", i.e. a horse-racing track. This was the part of St Benets Way, south of what is now the Racecourse Inn, Salhouse Road. The track continued west-south-westwards towards Norwich.

There was also a racetrack north of St William' chapel, on the north side of Mousehold Lane, in Sprowston (Plate 39). Kirkpatrick shows it on his 1720 plan of the chapel (see "Dussindale" above). Blomefield mentions it in 1745. He said St William's chapel "stood by the race-ground on Mushold-hill, where the road parts, between the starting-post and the lodge, on that side next the city." What this means is that, until the Sprowston part of Mousehold was enclosed in 1801, there was a road that diverged from what is now Mousehold Lane. By 1720 this road had been converted into a racetrack. The road left Mousehold Lane near its junction with the southern arm of Oak Tree Drive (The Great War Memorial Cottages). (This seems to be where the starting-post was). It then ran east-south-eastwards towards what is now Salhouse Road.

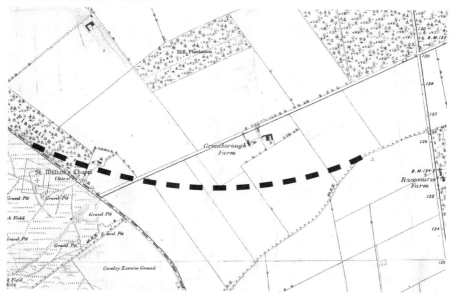

*Plate 39: The dashed line shows part of the suggested route of the 18th century racecourse between the site of St William's chapel, Mousehold Lane, and where the route joined the Thorpe boundary just west of Woodside Road (1880s Ordnance Survey map).*

It is very likely that the two racetracks were part of the same track. This means that for most of the 18th century there was a racetrack on Mousehold Heath that was almost two miles in length. It started just north of St William's chapel and ran east-south-eastwards until it crossed what is now Salhouse Road. It is clear from the 1600 Mousehold map, and another Mousehold map of 1624, that, shortly after crossing Salhouse Road, the road along which the track ran began to turn until it ran east-north-eastwards. It then met St Benet's Way near where Munnings Road meets Barclay Road. It continued along St Benets Way, the Sprowston / Thorpe boundary, probably as far as a point south of the Racecourse Inn, Salhouse Road. It appears from an advertisement for the "Norwich Races" beginning on Monday 22nd May 1738 that this was not the finishing point, but the turning point of the race. This is because each heat was four miles in length, the winner being the best horse over three heats.

Racing on Mousehold Heath was probably begun by Sir Lambert Blackwell shortly after he purchased the manor of Sprowston in 1714. Following his death in 1727, racing was probably continued by his son and heir, Sir Charles Blackwell. It reached a summit between 1738 and 1741 when the Norwich Races on Mousehold Heath were reported every year in the "Norwich Mercury". They were held on three successive days in Whit-week. Entertainment was provided by the Norwich Company of Comedians. In addition, for the duration of the meeting, there was cock-fighting at the Red Lion in Norwich, on the corner of Red Lion Street and Orford Hill.

In 1739 it was reported that the number of spectators was "above 40,000 on Wednesday when the Hunter's Purse was run for." The winner of that prize of forty guineas was "Mr Spicer's Grey Gelding, Carpenter". The rider wore white. Racing appears to have ceased following Sir Charles Blackwell's death in July 1741. There was an attempt at a revival in the late 1790s. In December 1799 it was reported that some officers garrisoned at the Cavalry Barracks had observed the "old practice" of running heats on Mousehold Heath.

Following enclosure in 1801, racing on the old course was no longer possible. However, there was racing on what had been Mousehold Heath in the years between 1838 and 1842 and again in 1848 and 1876. The races were instigated by John Harvey (see "Thorpe Lodge" above) and organised by officers at the Cavalry Barracks. In 1839 it was reported that "there was an oval course marked out by white posts upon a fine expanse of level turf." The 1841 tithe map shows two adjacent fields called "Old Race Course". They covered 56 acres and were adjacent to Woodside Road to the west and Plumstead Road East to the south. This is likely to have been the site of the 19th century racecourse. It is commemorated by the name Racecourse Road, off Woodside Road, previously Racecourse Farm. The 1848 race meeting took place "on land near the Heart's Ease Inn, Plumstead Road, Norwich". It is probably the same site.

The Racecourse Inn, Salhouse Road was not part of the 19th century racecourse. It is in Sprowston. In the 1840s it was a substantial house called the Grange that was owned by Sir Edward John Hardinge Stracey of Rackheath Hall. However, the building is only about 400 yards (366 metres) north of St Benets Way, the route of the 18th century racecourse, and near where the horses turned.

# Appendix 3 – Maps of Thorpe St Andrew in about 1600, about 1750 and 1800

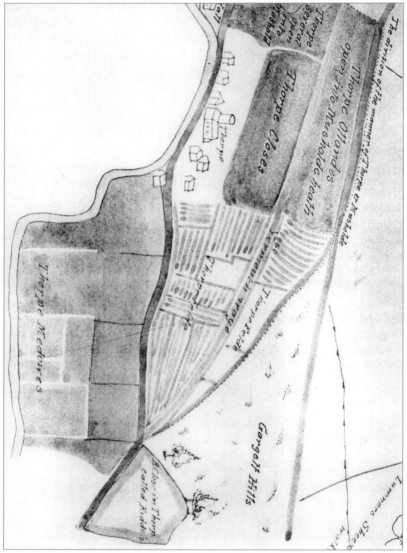

*Plate 40 : Thorpe St Andrew in about 1600 from a map of Mousehold Heath showing sheepwalks.*

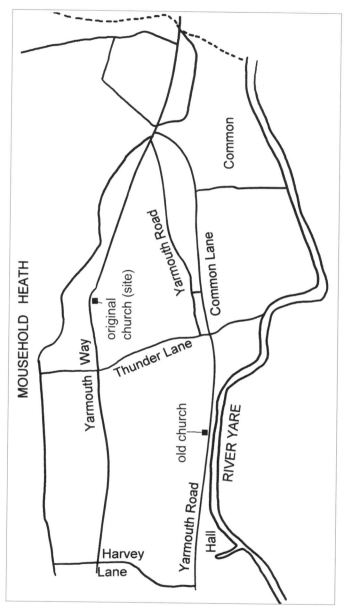

MOUSEHOLD HEATH

Common

Yarmouth Road

Common Lane

original
church (site)

Yarmouth Way

Thunder Lane

old church

RIVER YARE

Yarmouth Road

Hall

Harvey
Lane

*Plate 41: Thorpe St Andrew in about 1750, showing the extent of Mousehold Heath and the common in the 18th century and the road network as it was from the mid-16th century until 1769.*

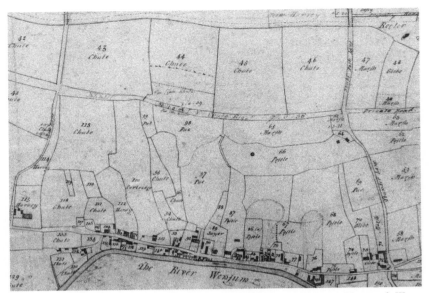

*Plate 42: Fields between Harvey Lane and Thunder Lane, showing Yarmouth Way just south of Mousehold Heath, from the 1800 enclosure map.*

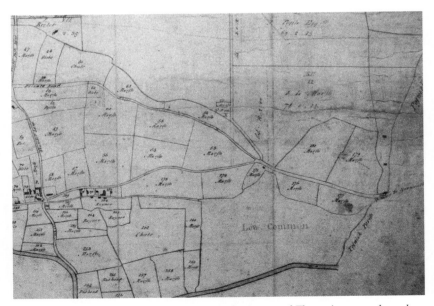

*Plate 43: Fields and common between Thunder Lane and Thorpe's eastern boundary from the 1800 enclosure map.*

154

*Plate 44: From Water Lane (next to 140 on the map) to the Rushcutters (146) from the 1800 enclosure map.*

# Appendix 4 - Sources

## Books

Aldous D W Unpublished notes of 1951-53 excavations of what until 1988 was thought to be "St Catherine's, Thorpe"

Allthorpe-Guyton M *John Thirtle (1777-1839) Drawings in Norwich Castle Museum* (1977)

Armstrong M J *History and antiquities of the county of Norfolk* (1781)

Ayers B *The Cathedral Site before 1096* in Atherton I and others (editors) *Norwich Cathedral - Church, City and Diocese 1096-1996* (1996)

Barton T F and Farrow M A (editors) *Index of wills proved in the Consistory Court of Norwich 1687-1750* Norfolk Record Society 34 (1965)

Batcock N *The Ruined and Deserted Churches of Norfolk* East Anglian Archaeology Report 51 (1991) (Microfiche ref.: St Andrew 1 - 9:F12; St Andrew 2 - 5:G9).

Blackwell L *A true and exact particular and inventory of all and singular the lands, tenements,,, and personal estate ..., which Sir Lambert Blackwell, Bart. ... was seis'd or possess'd of... upon 1 June 1720 ,,,* (1721)

Blake W J *Parson Russell's Reply to Blomefield's queries* Norfolk Archaeology xxix, 164-180 (1946)

Blomefield F *An essay towards a topographical history of the county of Norfolk* (1806)

Brett P *Edward Paston (1550-1630): a Norfolk gentleman and his musical collection* Trans. Cambridge Bibliographical Soc. 4, 51-64 (1964)

Bryant T H *The Churches of Norfolk No. CCCCLXXIV S. Andrew's, Thorpe Episcopi*, Norwich Mercury 28 December 1907 and 4 January 1908

Burstall E B *The Pastons and their manor of Binham* Norfolk Archaeology 30, (1952), 101-29

Butcher D *Lowestoft, 1550-1750: Development and Change in a*

*Suffolk Coastal Town* (2008)

Cannell E F *Norfolk County Mental Hospital – Engineering Department – "The Progress of a Century" 1814-1914* (typescript c.1914)

Carter A *The site of Dussindale* Norfolk Archaeology xxxix, 54-62 (1984)

[Chambers J] *Norfolk Tour* (1829)

Cherry S *Mental Health Care in Modern England; The Norfolk Lunatic Asylum / St Andrew's Hospital, 1810-1998* (2003)

Clifford D and Clifford T *John Crome* (1968)

Cotman A M and Hawcroft F W *Old Norwich – A Collection of Paintings, Prints and Drawings of an Ancient City* (1961)

Cozens-Hardy B (editor) *The diary of Sylas Neville, 1767-1788* (1950)

Dodwell B (editor) *The Charters of Norwich Cathedral Priory Part One* (1974)

*Eastern Daily Press* 16th April 1879 (Horsewater), 19th November 1895 (the Rushcutters)

*Eastern Evening News* 14th May 1957 (the present church), 13th August 1955 (Thompson's Folly), 20 December 1968 and 3 January 1969 (old doorways at Thorpe Lodge and Thorpe Hall)

Ewing W C *Notices of the Norwich merchant's marks* Norfolk Archaeology 3, (1852), 176-228

Farrow M A (editor) *Wills at Norwich 1370-1550* Norfolk Record Society 16 (1943-45)

Farrow M A and Barton T F (editors) *Index of wills proved in the Consistory Court of Norwich 1604-1686* Norfolk Record Society 28 (1958)

Fawcett T *Thorpe Water Frolic* Norfolk Archaeology xxxvi, 393-398 (1977)

Fawcett T *John Crome and the Idea of Mousehold* Norfolk Archaeology xxxviii, 168-181 (1982)

Goreham G *The history of Thorpe Hamlet, Norwich* unpublished typescript (1964*)*

Grigor J *The Eastern aboretum; or register of remarkable trees, seats, gardens etc. in the county of Norfolk* (1841)

(Hardy C) *Memories of Norwich and its inhabitants fifty years ago by a nonagenarian* (1888)

Harper-Bill C (editor) *English Episcopal Acta 21 – Norwich 1215-1243* (2000)

Harrison T *Postwick and relatives: written in the early part of the eighteenth century, by T Harrison of Great Plumstead* (1858)

Hayes R *The 'Private Life' of a Late Medieval Bishop: William Alnwick, Bishop of Norwich and Lincoln* in Rogers N (editor) *England in the Fifteenth Century* (1994)

Hughey R (editor) *The correspondence of Lady Katherine Paston 1603-1627* Norfolk Record Society 14 (1941)

Kelly G I *The King's Head Public House, 36 Yarmouth Road, Thorpe St Andrew – A history* (typescript 1987)

Kent E A *– Thorpe Hall –* paper read on Norfolk and Norwich Archaeological Society excursion in July 1927 – Norfolk Archaeology 23, (1928), xlvii- l

Kent E A and Stephenson A *Norwich Inheritance* (1948)

Kitson S D *The Life of John Sell Cotman* (1937)

MacCulloch D *A Reformation in the balance: power struggles in the diocese of Norwich, 1533-1553* in Rawcliffe C and others (editors) *Counties and Communities Essays on East Anglian History* (1996)

Marshall W *The Rural Economy of Norfolk* (1787)

Moore A *The Norwich School of Artists* (1985)

*Norfolk Chronicle* 3rd May 1800 and others 1800-1801(Enclosure), May 1814 (St Andrew's Park), 30th July 1864 (No. 42 Yarmouth Road), 2 June 1866 (the present church)

Norfolk and Norwich directories - various

*Norwich Mercury* 1738-1741 (Horse racing), 3rd May 1800, 4 April 1801 and others 1800-1801 (Enclosure), July 1841 (Thorpe Lodge), 9 July 1842 (the Rushcutters), 2 June 1866 (the present church), 28 December 1907 and 4 January 1908 (Bryant's *The churches of Norfolk*)

Pevsner N *The Buildings of England – North-East Norfolk and Norwich* (1962)

Rajnai M *The Norwich School of Painters* (1978)

Roberts V *Notes on the History of St Andrew's Hospital* (typescript

c. 1998)

Robinson B and Rose E J *Norfolk Origins 2: Roads and Tracks* (1983)

Rose E J and Davison A J *'St Catherine's Thorpe'- the Birth and Death of a Myth* Norfolk Archaeology xl, 179-181 (1988)

Rye W *Castles and manor houses from the Conquest to the present time* (1916)

Russell F W *Kett's Rebellion in Norfolk* (1859)

(Sawbridge M) *An account of Thorpe Hall, near Norwich, Norfolk* (c 1979)

Soros SW and Arbuthnot C *Thomas Jeckyll, Architect and Designer 1827-1881* (2003)

Sotherton N *The Commoyson in Norfolk 1549* written circa 1550-1560 (edited edition by Yaxley S, (1987))

Stark J *Scenery of the rivers of Norfolk, comprising the Yare, the Waveney, and the Bure...with historical and geological descriptions (by J W Robberds Esq.)* (1834)

Supple W R *A History of Thorpe-next-Norwich otherwise Thorpe Episcopi and Thorpe S. Andrew* (1917)

Tanner N P (editor) *Heresy trials in the diocese of Norwich, 1423-31* (1977)

Thomson D G *The Norfolk County Asylum, Thorpe, Norwich 1814-1903* (1903)

Thorpe St Andrew Parish Council *Snippets 1895-1995* (1995)

Walpole J *Art and Artists of the Norwich School* (1997)

Williams J F (editor) *Bishop Redman's visitation 1597* Norfolk Record Society 18 (1946)

Williamson T *The Origins of Norfolk* (1993)

Yaxley D and Virgoe N *The Manor House in Norfolk* (1978)

Young A *An inquiry into the propriety of applying wastes to the better maintenance and support of the poor: With instances of the great effects which have attended their acquisition of property, in keeping them from the parish even in the present scarcity. Being the substance of some notes taken in a tour in the year 1800* (1801)

Young A *General View of the Agriculture of the County of Norfolk* (1804)

# Maps

Sanctuary map of Norwich of 1541 in Kirkpatrick J *Streets and lanes of the city of Norwich* (1889)

Cuningham's map of Norwich 1558

Mousehold map of 1589 in Kirkpatrick J *Streets and lanes of the city of Norwich* (1889) (W Hudson, who edited the volume, stated incorrectly that the map was plotted in 1585)

Mousehold Heath showing sheepwalks, circa 1600 – Norfolk Record Office (NRO) MS 4460

A plot or description of part of Mousehold Heath lying in Thorpe next Pockthorpe, surveyed by Thomas Waterman, 1624 (NRO MS 4457/1-4)

Map of "the Fould Courses of Plumstead, Lumners Great Close and Fould Course, lying in Plumstead, Sprowston and Thorp" by William Cooke of Tharston, Surveyor, 1718 (NRO CHC 11913)

John Kirkpatrick's "Plan of the Churchyard & Precinct of the Chappel of St William in the Wood near Norwich", circa 1720 - in Goulburn E M, Symonds H and Hailstone E *The ancient sculptures in the roof of Norwich Cathedral, which exhibit the course of scripture history... to which is added a history of the see of Norwich from its foundation to the dissolution of the monasteries* (1876)

Sketch maps of certain tithable land in common field and meadow of between 1700 and 1731 (NRO PD228/51)

1767 Plan and survey of River Wensum [Yare] and riparian owners - NRO Case 16e 108/109

Faden's map of Norfolk surveyed 1790-94 and printed 1797, in Barringer J C *An introduction to Faden's map of Norfolk* Norfolk Record Society 42 (1975)

1800 Draft Inclosure Map of the whole parish of Thorpe - R Chasteney –NRO BR 276/1/0684 (The key to the numbering used in the map is in NRO BR 90/3/4)

Sketch of the Old Inclosures in Thorpe [1800] NRO BR 276/1/0534; 1801 Thorpe enclosure map, showing allotments of Mousehold Heath (NRO N/TC 50/6) circa 1817 Ordnance survey map (sketch map of Norwich)

1819 Plan of Roads in Thorpe, R Pratt, Surveyor – NRO BR 276/1/0453

1824 Map of County and City of Norwich, Woodrow and Newton surveyors – NRO N/TC 62/1

1825 Map of rivers from Norwich to Reedham, with names of owners of adjacent lands - NRO MC 103/47

Undated 19th century Thorpe St Andrew estate map: estate of Thomas Batley – NRO DS 340

1841 Thorpe Tithe map with 1842 Tithe apportionment – NRO 596

1861 Enclosure map for Thorpe Low Common with enclosure award – NRO/C/ Sca/292

Ordnance Survey 25 inch maps of the 1880s and later

## Manuscript sources in Norfolk Record Office

Rye Manuscripts (4691/80A Z3F) – papers regarding lecture about Thorpe, including note about Counsels' Opinions on rights over green 1757 and 1766.

Rye Manuscripts 6 Norris volumes 2 and 5 (also MF 569-70)

Manor of Postwick and Great Plumstead, field book, 1576 (MC 1817/12, 843X5)

Lease Ledger 1798-1809 (DCN 47/16)

Sprowston Estate leases 1509-1863 (DCN 49/50)

Libellum de mensuracione Bosci de Thorp inter dominum Episcopum et Priorem (DCN 51/111) (13th century (?) book of measurement of the wood of Thorpe between the Lord Bishop and the Prior)

Sprowston estate papers 1713 (DCN 59/31)

PD 228 - Parish documents of Thorpe Episcopi or Thorpe-next-Norwich

/39 Glebe terriers 1763-1955

/51 Sequestrators' accounts 1670; Tithe accounts 1700-1731, including two small sketch maps of land in common field and meadow

/76 Churchwardens' accounts and Vestry minutes 1745-1875

/111 Town House (i.e. Church House) Declaration of Trust 1587

/112 Town House: copy of conveyance to new trustees 1704

/114 Papers re sale of Town House
/149 List of owners and tenants of commonages at Thorpe 1741
/151 Thorpe inclosure; settlement of claims 1800; notice under award to John Harvey 1801; letter re boundaries between hamlet and parish 1808
/152 Agreement between Sir Roger Kerrison, John Harvey, Jehoshaphat Postle and other landowners re use of Low Common, 1803
/153 Sale particulars of estate in Thorpe and Carrow 1810; of estate in Thorpe 1815
Abstracts of title including estate of John Harvey deceased 1675-1842 – MC 1940/3, 895x8
Thorpe Lodge sale particulars 1842 – MC 860
Glebe terriers 1621-1753 (DN/TER/148/3/1-32)
Manorial Court Rolls of Thorpe-next-Norwich with Plumstead 1721-1841 (MF/X/163/7 and MF/X/233/7 and 8)
St Andrew's Hospital, Thorpe - records (SAH)

**Other sources**

Census Returns 1841-1901
Norfolk Historic Environment Record
www.jjhc.info/blakistonharriotharvey1886.htm - information about Harriot Blakiston née Harvey (2014)
www.sothebys.com/it/auctions/ecatalogue/lot.pdf.L09637.html/f/237/L09637-237.pdf - 2009 sale notice of Thomas Bardwell's "A Prospect of Trowse Hall, Norwich" (2014)

# Postscript and Acknowledgements

The first edition of this book was published in 2002 under the title "Thorpe St Andrew - A History".

This second edition contains many revisions. In particular, it has been updated in the light of new discoveries, such as the 1800 enclosure map and Bardwell's 1760 painting. In addition, a new section on Mousehold Heath has been included, as it used to comprise just over half of the parish. As it used to be part of Mousehold, I have also described the origins of what is now Lion Wood.

Kett's Rebellion came to an end at the battle of Dussindale on Tuesday 27th August 1549. In this book further thought has been given to where Dussindale was and where, on the border between Thorpe St Andrew and Sprowston, the battle took place.

As Miss Janet Smith of Thorpe St Andrew was the inspiration for the first edition of this book, I would like to thank her again. Her archive collection is now held by Thorpe St Andrew Town Council. I would also like to thank Catherine Ellis for her comments on the draft of this book. In addition, I have been grateful for the assistance of the staff of the Norfolk Heritage Centre and the Norfolk Record Office.

I am grateful to all those who have supplied me with photographs for this book. Several of them are from my own postcard collection. The original provenance of some of them has been difficult to establish. Plates 4, 12, 14, 20, 26 and 33 have been reproduced by courtesy of the Norfolk Heritage Centre. Plates 21 and 31 have been reproduced by courtesy of Mrs Vivienne Roberts. Plate 17 has been reproduced by courtesy of the Norwich Castle Museum & Art Gallery. Plate 23 has been reproduced by courtesy of Mr Nigel C C Bill. The map reproduced as Plate 40 in Appendix 3 and copies of parts of the 1800 enclosure map have been included by courtesy of the Norfolk Record Office.

**Trevor Nuthall**